Newman: The Heart of Holiness

ALSO BY RODERICK STRANGE

Newman and the Gospel of Christ
The Catholic Faith
Living Catholicism
The Risk of Discipleship: The Catholic Priest Today
John Henry Newman: A Mind Alive
(ed.) John Henry Newman: A Portrait in Letters

NEWMAN:
The Heart of Holiness

RODERICK STRANGE

HODDER &
STOUGHTON

First published in Great Britain in 2019 by Hodder & Stoughton
An Hachette UK company

1

Copyright © Roderick Strange, 2019

The right of Roderick Strange to be identified as the Author of the Work has been
asserted by him in accordance with the Copyright, Designs and Patents Act 1988.

All Scriptural references are taken from translations
used in Newman's texts with his emphases.

A CIP catalogue record for this title is available from the British Library.

Hardback ISBN 978 1 529 36261 9
eBook ISBN 978 1 529 36260 2

Typeset in Bembo MT by Hewer Text UK Ltd, Edinburgh
Printed and bound in Great Britain by Clays Ltd, Elcograf S.p.A.

Hodder & Stoughton policy is to use papers that are natural, renewable
and recyclable products and made from wood grown in sustainable
forests. The logging and manufacturing processes are expected to
conform to the environmental regulations of the country of origin.

Hodder & Stoughton Ltd
Carmelite House
50 Victoria Embankment
London EC4Y 0DZ

www.hodderfaith.com

In Memory of

Geoffrey Rowell

1943–2017

Contents

Abbreviations

The abbreviations I have used are those which have become standard and are listed in C. S. Dessain et al (eds), *The Letters and Diaries of John Henry Newman* i–xxxii (Oxford and London, 1961–2007); hereafter *L.D.* Where a second reference to a letter is given in square brackets, it is to be found in Roderick Strange (ed.), *John Henry Newman: A Portrait in Letters* (Oxford, 2015, 2019).

Page references are taken from the Uniform Edition of Newman's works. Where a second reference is given in square brackets, it is taken from a subsequent critical edition, noted below.

Apo.	*Apologia pro Vita Sua*
Ari.	*The Arians of the Fourth Century*
Ath. i, ii	*Select Treatises of St Athanasius*
A.W.	*Autobiographical Writings*
D.A.	*Discussions and Arguments on Various Subjects*
Dev.	*An Essay on the Development of Christian Doctrine*
Diff. i, ii	*Certain Difficulties Felt by Anglicans in Catholic Teaching*
Ess. i, ii	*Essays Critical and Historical*
G.A.	*An Essay in Aid of a Grammar of Assent*
H.S. i, ii, iii	*Historical Sketches*
Idea	*The Idea of a University Defined and Illustrated*
Jfc.	*Lectures on the Doctrine of Justification*
M.D.	*Meditations and Devotions of the Late Cardinal Newman*

Mix.	*Discourses Addressed to Mixed Congregations*
O.S.	*Sermons Preached on Various Occasions*
P.S. i–viii	*Parochial and Plain Sermons*
Prepos.	*Present Position of Catholics in England*
S.D.	*Sermons Bearing on Subjects of the Day*
T.T.	*Tracts Theological and Ecclesiastical*
U.S.	*Fifteen Sermons Preached Before the University of Oxford*
V.M. i, ii	*The Via Media*
V.V.	*Verses on Various Occasions*

Critical Editions

Martin J. Svalgic (ed.), *Apologia pro Vita Sua* (Oxford, 1967).

Ian T. Ker (ed.), *An Essay in Aid of a Grammar of Assent* (Oxford, 1985).

Ian T. Ker (ed.), *The Idea of a University* (Oxford, 1976).

H. D. Weidner (ed.), *The 'Via Media' of the Anglican Church* (Oxford, 1990).

James Edward Earnest and Gerard Tracey (eds), *Fifteen Sermons Preached Before the University of Oxford* (Oxford, 2006).

Significant events in Newman's life

21 February 1801	Birth
August– December 1816	First religious conversion
8 June 1817	Goes up to Trinity College, Oxford
30 November 1817	First Communion in Trinity College Chapel
November 1820	BA degree
12 April 1822	Elected a fellow of Oriel
13 June 1824	Ordained an Anglican deacon
29 May 1825	Ordained an Anglican priest
26 November 1827	Collapses while examining at Oxford
5 January 1828	His sister Mary dies
14 March 1828	Instituted as Vicar of St Mary the Virgin, Oxford
15 June 1830	Accepts his removal as a tutor at Oriel
December 1832– July 1833	Mediterranean journey, becoming ill in Sicily in May
14 July 1833	Keble preaches the Assize Sermon on 'National Apostasy'; Newman regards it as the start of the Oxford Movement
9 September 1833	The first of the *Tracts for the Times* is published
21 July 1835	Newman's mother lays the first stone of the Littlemore church
17 May 1836	Death of Mrs Newman

22 September 1836	Consecration of the new church at Littlemore
11 March 1837	Publication of the *Lectures on the Prophetical Office*
9 April 1837	Weekly early Eucharist at St Mary's begins
July–August 1839	Begins reading about the Monophysite heresy
27 February 1841	*Tract 90* controversy begins
13 November 1841	Protests against the Jerusalem bishopric
9 February 1842	Moves to Littlemore
4 May 1842	His growing conviction about the Roman Catholic Church
25 September 1843	Preaches his final Anglican sermon, 'The Parting of Friends'
29 September 1843	Estranged from his sister, Harriett
1845	Writes his *Essay on the Development of Christian Doctrine*
3 October 1845	Resigns his Oriel fellowship
9 October 1845	Received into the Catholic Church
22 February 1846	Leaves Littlemore for Maryvale, near Oscott
28 October 1846	Arrives in Rome
30 May 1847	Ordained as a Catholic priest
28 June 1847	Enters the Oratorian noviciate
24 December 1847	Arrives back in London
1 February 1848	Establishes the English Oratory
14 February 1848	Admits Frederick Faber and his companions to the Oratory
31 October 1848	Moves to St Wilfrid's, Cotton
2 February 1849	The opening of the Oratory in Alcester Street, Birmingham
31 May 1849	The opening of the London Oratory
28 July 1851	Denounces Achilli in a lecture on Catholicism in England and is sued for libel

12 November 1851	Appointed Rector of the Catholic University in Ireland
16 February 1852	Moves to the new Oratory house in Edgbaston
10 May–7 June 1852	Delivers first five Discourses on University Education
12–24 June 1852	The Achilli trial; he is found guilty for not proving his charges
16 July 1852	His sister Harriett dies
August 1852	His aunt, Elizabeth, dies
21 July–20 November 1852	Composes the remaining Discourses on University Education
31 January 1853	Sentenced in the Achilli trial to a fine of £100
4 June 1854	Installed as Rector of the Catholic University in Dublin
1855–1856	Breakdown of the relationship between the two Oratories
12 January–4 February 1856	Visits Rome because of the breakdown
27 August 1857	Receives the invitation to oversee a new translation of the Bible
12 November 1858	Resigns as Rector of the Dublin University
21 March 1859	Agrees to edit *The Rambler*
2 May 1859	Opens the Oratory School
22 May 1859	Bishop Ullathorne asks Newman to resign as editor of *The Rambler*
July 1859	Writes in his second issue 'On Consulting the Faithful in Matters of Doctrine' and is denounced to Rome for heresy
5 December 1861–24 January 1862	Crisis at the Oratory School when Nicholas Darnell seeks total control, and

	then resigns with other members of staff, but the crisis is resolved before the beginning of the new term
30 December 1863	Learns of Kingsley's slur against him in *Macmillan's Magazine*
February–June 1864	The *Apologia* controversy with Kingsley
23 August 1864	Offered the Catholic mission at Oxford and buys a site
end of December	Opposition and disapproval ends the project and the site is sold
May and June 1865	Publication of *The Dream of Gerontius*
31 January 1866	Publication of his *Letter to Pusey*
May 1867	Ambrose St John in Rome finally resolves the misunderstanding concerning Newman's article in *The Rambler*
18 August 1867	After first accepting, Newman declines a second offer to undertake the mission in Oxford, as he would not be allowed to reside there
8 December 1869	Opening of the First Vatican Council
15 March 1870	Publication of *A Grammar of Assent*
18 July 1870	Definition of papal infallibility
20 October 1870	Pope Pius IX suspends indefinitely the First Vatican Council
14 January 1875	Publication of *A Letter to the Duke of Norfolk*, in controversy with Gladstone
14 December 1877	Invited to become an Honorary Fellow of Trinity College, Oxford
7 February 1878	Death of Pope Pius IX
20 February 1878	Election of Pope Leo XIII
31 January 1879	Offered the cardinalate
15 May 1879	Receives the cardinal's hat at a public consistory
11 August 1890	Dies of pneumonia

Preface

'I have nothing of a Saint about me'

On 11 February 1850, John Henry Newman wrote to a Miss G. Munro. She had been received into the Catholic Church by Nicholas Wiseman, the future Cardinal, five years earlier, and Newman had become her spiritual director. He wrote to her for many years. On this occasion he was returning a letter she had sent on to him from Elizabeth Moore.

Elizabeth Moore, who later became a nun, was deeply impressed by Newman. In her letter she had spoken of him as a saint. Newman was having none of it and wanted her undeceived. 'I have nothing of a Saint about me as everyone knows,' he declared, 'and it is a severe (and salutary) mortification to be thought next door to one.' Then he went on, 'I may have a high view of many things, but it is the consequence of education and of a peculiar cast of intellect – but this is very different from *being* what I admire. I have no tendency to be a saint – it is a sad thing to say.' This is the well-known letter in which he observed, 'Saints are not literary men, they do not love the classics, they do not write Tales.' And he concluded, 'It is enough for me to black the saints' shoes – if St Philip [Neri, founder of the oratory and his patron] uses blacking, in heaven' (*L.D.* xiii, p. 419 [246]). Nevertheless, in spite of this typically diffident self-appraisal, the Church has decided otherwise and declared Newman to be a saint after all.

Before canonisation, however, there had to be beatification. Newman was beatified on 19 September 2010 by Pope Benedict XVI during his visit to the United Kingdom, one hundred and twenty years after Newman's death. Some people found the delay incomprehensible, but there had been a particular obstacle to overcome.

To begin with, it is important to remember that those who are canonised are not being acclaimed as holier than those who have been beatified. Comparative judgments are completely out of place. Holiness is holiness. The distinction between them lies elsewhere. Both are being held up as examples of Christian life that can be followed with confidence, but those called 'Blessed' are being offered as models for a particular place or country, while those who are named as saints are being acknowledged as models for the universal Church. As a process it is entirely natural, especially in countries like Italy and Spain where Catholic culture is deeply rooted. It makes sense to inquire whether a person had a reputation for sanctity in their local area where they were well known personally, before going on to investigate whether there was evidence of more widespread admiration and devotion.

When Newman died, however, in 1890, in spite of various more personal controversies relating to his ministry, he had been living modestly and unostentatiously in Birmingham for more than forty years. Since 1879 he had been a cardinal and so was admired and esteemed, but the local people were not going to be making a fuss about him. That wasn't their style any more than it was his. When he died, thousands attended his funeral, but the English Midlands was hardly a setting in which someone was likely to acquire what might be regarded as a reputation for sanctity.

Newman has been valued in England, but the English tend to be undemonstrative. The local scene was becalmed. On the other hand, internationally his influence has been profound. Scholars in France and Germany, in Spain and Italy, in the Netherlands and Belgium, in Australia and the United States, have been studying his life and writings. A Newman industry has been flourishing for decades. In addition, there has been an ever-increasing stream of people coming from abroad to visit the Birmingham Oratory, which he founded and which was his home for so long. They came because of their devotion to him. So, while the local scene was becalmed, the international scene, the universal scene, was bursting with life and energy. It is a great irony that the Church's normal, sensible procedure had in a way put the brakes on his recognition.

★

My own interest in Newman goes back to 1964. Since then, in spite of other commitments, I have often been reading his works, reflecting on his life and studying and writing about him. Some years before his beatification in 2010 – and, in truth, without giving that a thought – I decided to see whether I could organise some of that material – articles I had written and lecture notes for talks – into a book. It was not intended as an exhaustive study, nor was I pretending that Newman was always right about everything, but it was a way for me to acknowledge my debt to him, and I hoped that, by indicating his influence on me, I could open up paths for other people to understand him too.

The book was published in 2008 as *John Henry Newman: A Mind Alive* and was received well. I was particularly gratified when a priest wrote to thank me. He said that he had always been told that Newman was significant, but had never really been able to understand why until he read the book. It was, of course, precisely the reaction I had hoped for.

Since the beatification, more material has come together and, with Newman declared to be a saint, it occurs to me that there is something further to be added. For a long time I have thought of holiness as code for the inner life of God, so my interest here is not so much in what Newman had to say on a variety of subjects – such as the Blessed Virgin Mary, or doctrinal development, or the laity. My interest is rather in his own interior life – in his intimacy with God, in his understanding of Christ, in contemplation, in prayer and his experience of darkness, in the dark night of his soul – an interior life that was not reclusive, but became the basis for his ministry, serving others. This book, therefore, is an attempt to peel back the layers of his spirituality so as to explore respectfully the heart of his holiness.

By way of introduction, a useful place to begin may be, unusually, at the end.

★

Newman died on 11 August 1890. Three years later, William Neville, a priest of the Birmingham Oratory who had been Newman's assistant and chaplain in the final years of his life, published a collection called *Meditations and Devotions*. It contained some of the reflections and prayers Newman had composed for his own use over the years. We will be noticing some of them in this book. But I mention them now because Neville states in his introduction that Newman used to say he prayed or meditated best 'with a pen in his hand' (*M.D.* p. ix). There is a famous saying: 'Pray as you can, not as you can't.' People need to discover the way of praying that suits them best: for some, that is reflective reading; for others, it is to recite prayers or to sing psalms; for others again, it means utter silence. There are many ways of praying. But Newman believed he prayed best with a pen in his hand.

What might that mean? Praying with a pen in your hand may suggest prayer as a rather detached, cerebral exercise. What is written down may seem to be kept at arm's length. Yet Newman's prayerfulness inspired and found expression in his sermons, which stirred those who heard them. W. G. Ward is one example. He was a gifted pure mathematician and philosopher and one-time fellow of Balliol College, and later came to disagree fiercely with Newman on theological matters. At first he had taken no interest in the Tractarian Movement of which Newman was a leader. (The Tractarians were seeking to

restore the Catholic tradition within the Church of England.)
Urged to hear Newman preach in St Mary the Virgin, Oxford's
university church, Ward had dismissed the notion out of hand:
'Why should I go and listen to such myths?'[1] But, once
persuaded to hear him, Ward's life was changed, so much so
that in those early days he became one of Newman's most
ardent disciples. And many years later, even after he had
adopted extreme views and clashed with Newman, he nevertheless told him that their differences made him feel 'a kind of
intellectual orphan'.[2]

And then there is Matthew Arnold's famous description of
Newman preaching in St Mary the Virgin on Sunday
afternoons:

> Who could resist the charm of that spiritual apparition, gliding
> in the dim afternoon light through the aisles of St. Mary's,
> rising into the pulpit, and then, in the most entrancing of
> voices, breaking the silence with words and thoughts which
> were a religious music – sweet, subtle, mournful? I seem to
> hear him still . . .[3]

Ward and Arnold, two very different people, are among many
who have borne witness to the power of Newman's preaching.
They were moved by him. Their hearts were touched.
Newman may have prayed with a pen in his hand, but those
prayers cannot have been dry and lifeless. In the words of James
Anthony Froude, also describing Newman in St Mary's pulpit:
'I had then never seen so impressive a person . . . He told us

1 Wilfrid Ward, *William George Ward and the Oxford Movement* (London:
Macmillan & Co., 1889), p. 80.
2 Ward, *William George Ward and the Oxford Movement*, p. 81.
3 Matthew Arnold, 'Emerson', in R. H. Super (ed.), *Philistinism in
England and America* (Ann Arbor: University of Michigan Press, 1974),
p. 165.

what he believed to be true . . . No one who heard his sermons in those days can ever forget them.'⁴ We may conclude that he touched the hearts of others because, when he spoke, what he said came from the depths of his own heart, 'what he believed to be true'.

Newman's cardinal's motto, *Cor ad cor loquitur*, 'Heart speaks to heart', was a reality he had recognised very early. However, because what he wrote he wrote for others, because what he published was almost invariably in response to some need or particular occasion, that personal connection with what he was writing can pass unnoticed, camouflaged perhaps by the issues he was addressing.

★

As an Anglican, Newman had seen the Church of England as a branch of the Church Catholic – Roman, Eastern and Anglican – and he had championed it as a middle way between Protestant error and Roman excess. He came in time to qualify that notion, losing his faith in Anglicanism and becoming a Catholic. But he remained wedded instinctively to the moderation of the middle way. As a Catholic, too, he sought steadfastly to walk a path between error and excess.

Early in his life Newman had had a kind of evangelical conversion, imprinting in his heart, as he was to say, 'the thought of two and two only absolute and luminously self-evident beings, myself and my Creator' (*Apo*. p. 4 [17–18]). He was recognising the intimate link between the visible and the invisible worlds, between what is seen and what is unseen. For him, of course, that link was revealed supremely in Jesus of Nazareth, the Word made flesh. Awareness of that link, of Jesus

4 See J. A. Froude, Short Studies iv, pp. 278–84; quoted in Paul Chavasse, 'Newman the Preacher', in Philippe Lefebvre and Colin Mason (eds), *John Henry Newman: In His Time* (Oxford: Family Publications, 2007), p. 127.

as the Christ, made him alert to Christ's presence. When he preached, he urged those who heard him to be on the watch for Christ, a disposition he regarded as the very definition of what it means to be a Christian.

We may ask, therefore, who is the Christ for whom we should be watching? And, according to Newman, we should reflect not only on how the Christ is to be understood, but also on his presence in those who believe. Moreover, the Christ who was present on earth two thousand years ago remains, Newman was convinced, present now in the Eucharist, a gift that filled him with wonder and prompted his fidelity to prayer.

At the same time, being faithful was no safeguard against being tested. And so it will be instructive as well to explore his dark days, when people and events seemed to pummel and frustrate him. All the same, his instinct was consistently pastoral, both as a priest and because of his passion for education. He has left the Church a rich legacy.

Writers of books like this know that they are not alone. I am immensely grateful to Andy Lyon and his colleagues at Hodder for the help they have given me. I wish in particular to thank Caroline Michel, who has been my friend for many years and now, as my agent, has consistently offered me wise, professional advice and warm encouragement. Other friends, John Breen and Paul Murray OP, have once again cast patient and perceptive eyes over what I have written, supporting me yet alerting me as well to errors and failings. And then there is the legion of Newman scholars whom I have come to know and admire over the years and from whom I have learnt so much. There are too many to name, so let me name one to represent all the others: Geoffrey Rowell.

Geoffrey and I first met probably in 1972, just before he became a fellow of Keble College, Oxford. He was one of the examiners of my doctorate in 1974 and, soon after I returned to Oxford to the Catholic chaplaincy in 1977, he asked me to teach a Newman class with him. We taught together for eleven years. Later, from 1998 to 2015, while I was the Rector of the Beda College in Rome and when Geoffrey, by then the Anglican Bishop of Gibraltar, was visiting Rome, we would meet. I saw him last in 2015, at St Mary's University, Twickenham, when he came to the launch of a volume of Newman letters I had edited, *John Henry Newman: A Portrait in Letters*. Then the cancer that he had earlier overcome returned and overcame him, and he died in June 2017. We had been friends for forty years. Events made it impossible for me to attend his funeral, but some messages I received afterwards spoke of our long friendship and described me as one of his best-respected friends and colleagues. I feel humbled to be thought of in those terms. He would have been overjoyed by Newman's canonisation. I give thanks for our friendship and dedicate this book to his memory.

I

Newman's journey

Newman was born into a conventionally devout Anglican family in 1801. From an early age he was recognised as exceptionally gifted intellectually, but as a student at Oxford he worked too hard and almost collapsed when taking his final exams. He obtained a very poor degree. Nevertheless, a little more than a year later he sat other examinations, competing to become a fellow of Oriel College, and was elected in April 1822.

Oriel at that time was regarded academically as the most prestigious college in Oxford. Its senior common room was said to 'stink of logic'. That Newman, in the wake of virtual failure as an undergraduate, should have been elected so soon to such a society was an outstanding achievement. The provost of Oriel at the time, Edward Copleston, remarked many years later that Newman was 'not even a good classical scholar, yet in mind and powers of composition, and in taste and knowledge, he was decidedly superior' to others seeking election (*A.W.* p. 64). Although by nature tending to be reserved, Newman flourished at Oriel, coming out of his shell and revelling in exercising his intellectual gifts.

He was appointed as a tutor. In those days, tutors were expected to lecture to undergraduates indiscriminately, irrespective of their calibre. Newman regarded that approach as inadequate. He believed that talented undergraduates needed more individual tuition and that tutoring should involve moreover a moral or a pastoral dimension. A view that today would

be taken for granted was then regarded as radical. Oriel's provost, Copleston's successor, Edward Hawkins, disagreed with
Newman's line. Before long, no more pupils were being
appointed to him. And that lack of a teaching commitment led
to an unexpected turn of events.

In November 1827, while invigilating examinations,
Newman became unwell. Stress created by overwork, family
worries and College business caused him to collapse. And then
early in the new year, on 5 January, Mary, his enchanting
youngest sister, died. Illness and bereavement forced him to
consider more carefully what really mattered to him: was it
intellectual or moral excellence? And, at that time, he was
acquiring new friends at Oriel, notably John Keble, Edward
Pusey and Hurrell Froude.

Although Newman had undergone a kind of evangelical
conversion in 1816, these friends gradually led him from that
earlier, more earnest, evangelical Anglican stance to appreciate
the Catholic tradition within the Church of England. The
Anglican Church, of course, is characterised by comprehensive-
ness, by the way it seeks to include a wide range of traditions,
from Protestant evangelicalism through a kind of liberal rationalism to a high Catholic position. In those days, however, the
Catholic tradition within Anglicanism had rather been in decline.

When, in 1833, Newman and his friends perceived Parliament
to be interfering unduly, as they believed, in the affairs of the
Church, reorganising, however reasonably from another viewpoint, dioceses in Ireland, they resisted on principle and sought
to restore to the Church of England the Catholic tradition that
seemed to have been lost. This was the start of what became
known as the Oxford or Tractarian Movement. It was called
Tractarian because it spread its views initially by producing
short pamphlets or tracts (which later became much more
substantial).

The fact that Newman had no pupils to teach meant he had
the time and the energy to give himself wholeheartedly to the

cause and its work. Moreover, irony upon irony, Hawkins, before his election as Provost, had been the vicar of St Mary the Virgin, the university church. Newman was appointed in his place, so now, besides being freed from teaching undergraduates, he had that influential pulpit from which to preach. Those sermons that made their mark, as we have noticed, even on men as different as W. G. Ward and Matthew Arnold, have been acclaimed time and time again. Professor Owen Chadwick's comment is typical of many: 'It is of the essence of the [Oxford] Movement that its best writing should be enshrined in parochial sermons.'[1]

★

Full of energy and with time to spare, Newman threw himself into expounding his understanding of the Church of England. He understood it to be a branch of the Church Catholic: Roman, Eastern and Anglican. In his *Lectures on the Prophetical Office of the Church* in 1837, he described it not as infallible, because he regarded infallibility as a mark of the Church as one, which was no longer the case, but as indefectible, guided in other words to teach essential, saving truth indefectibly (see *V.M.* i, pp. 201, 190 [228, 219]). That truth, he explained, was to be found in Scripture and the Church of the Fathers and was what had been taught always, everywhere, and by everyone – *quod semper, quod ubique, quod ab omnibus* – as the Creed for admission into the Church and as the rule of subsequent teaching (see *V.M.* i, p. 222 [245]).

This essential teaching had been handed down in the Creed from bishop to bishop and so was called episcopal tradition, while there was another tradition, larger and less formal, that pervaded the Church 'like an atmosphere', interpreting revelation and unfolding its mysteries; this tradition he called 'prophetical' (see *V.M.* i, pp. 249–51 [267–9]).

1 Owen Chadwick, *The Mind of the Oxford Movement* (London: A. & C. Black, 1960), p. 42.

That, in brief, was the way he understood the Church of England and, at the same time, he presented this Anglican position as a middle way, a *via media*, between Protestant error on the one hand and Roman excess on the other. By 'excess' he meant the additions which he believed the Church of Rome had made to the original deposit of faith, such as the teaching about purgatory and the devotion paid to the Blessed Virgin and the saints. For some years he was untroubled and full of confidence, but then further study and certain events caused him to call into question the very position for which he had been so fervent a champion.

Precedents were important for Newman. He was conscious from the start that the *via media* was what he called 'a paper religion'. It had never seriously been tried. But then, during the summer of 1839, while studying the history of the Monophysites, he became aware that there was perhaps a precedent, but not as the middle way he was championing between error and extravagance. He suddenly saw Monophysitism, too, as charting a middle course: between Rome on the one hand and evident heresy, Eutychianism, on the other. However, it had itself been declared unorthodox, merely a way that, though less extreme, compromised and so colluded with error. How secure could a *via media* be?

Rome all the while had been the consistent bastion of orthodoxy. The middle way seemed to have crumbled beneath him. He saw his own position reflected in Monophysitism – not its teachings, but its temporising ecclesiology. 'I saw my face in that mirror,' he was to write later, 'and I was a Monophysite' (*Apo.* p. 114 [108]). And then a friend showed him an article on Anglicanism, written by Nicholas Wiseman. Wiseman at that time was Rector of the English College in Rome, and Newman had met him there in 1833. What startled Newman was a phrase of St Augustine's, *Securus judicat orbis terrarum*, which he translated as, 'The universal church is in its judgments secure of truth' (*Ess.* ii, p. 101). It kept ringing in his

4

ears: 'By those great words of the ancient Father, interpreting and summing up the long and varied course of ecclesiastical history, the theory of the *Via Media* was absolutely pulverized' (*Apo.* pp. 116–17 [110–11]). He thought, 'The Church of Rome will be found right after all' (*Apo.* p. 118 [111]).

After a while, however, he was at peace again. But two years later, in 1841, while studying Arianism, he found the Semi-Arians, like the Monophysites, replicating the same middle course between Rome and heresy. What was he to do?

Wrestling with these concerns, he sought to reinforce his position by writing *Tract 90*, which proved to be the last of the tracts. He wanted to demonstrate that there was, after all, compatibility between disputed Anglican and Catholic teaching. When the Thirty-nine Articles, the basis of the Elizabethan Settlement, had been formulated in 1559, the Council of Trent had not yet ended. As it only came to a close in 1563, the Articles could not be regarded as a response to the Council's teaching. Moreover, the Articles were in any case intended to include everyone, Catholics as well as Reformers, so that now, he argued, 'Catholics will not be excluded' (*V.M.* ii, pp. 347–8).

Newman did not expect the Tract to receive much attention, but it did. In particular he found that the episcopal opposition to it was overwhelming. He had seen his argument as supportive of the Anglican bishops' ministry, but he felt their reaction undermined the case that he was making for them. And then, shortly afterwards, he was appalled by a scheme to establish a bishopric in Jerusalem for non-Catholics, a post to be held alternately by an Anglican and a Lutheran or Calvinist. To him that arrangement seemed to equate Anglicanism with Protestantism and therefore identify it as simply another Protestant denomination. 'From the end of 1841,' he declared in his *Apologia*, 'I was on my death-bed, as regards my membership of the Anglican Church, though at the time I became aware of it only by degrees' (*Apo.* p. 147 [137]).

What was he to do? He was not a Protestant. The Anglicanism in which he believed, that middle way between error and excess, was being taken from him. Could it be the case perhaps that what hitherto he had regarded as Roman excesses, those additions to the deposit of faith, were not excesses after all, but authentic developments of living truth? He set himself to explore that possibility by studying doctrinal development, which he described as a 'hypothesis to account for a difficulty' (*Dev*. p. 30).

He proceeded slowly. It took him years, not months. But when he was convinced, he was received into the Catholic Church. That was on 9 October 1845. As he had explained ten months earlier, in December 1844 to his sister Jemima, who was bewildered and distressed at the turn her brother's life was taking, he was not motivated by disappointment or restlessness or some particular theory, nor was he being carried away by party spirit or influenced by admirers. He told her, 'As time goes by and persons have the opportunity of knowing me better, . . . they will be led to see that my motive simply is that I believe the Roman Church to be true' (*L.D.* x, p. 467 [200]).

The priest who received him was Dominic Barberi, an Italian Passionist who had long been driven by a deep desire to work in England. He is perhaps most famous for receiving Newman. For Newman, becoming a Catholic at such a time, when Catholics were a despised minority, meant sacrificing a position of honour and distinction, as a fellow of Oriel, as vicar of the university church and as a leader of the Oxford Movement, and it involved a parting from friends which only long years and goodwill on both sides would overcome.

The common reaction to his conversion has been captured succinctly by his biographer, Sheridan Gilley: 'Other Anglicans would never understand Newman's voluntary exile from that other Eden of the Establishment, from the golden world of the Anglican episcopal palace and deanery and public school.' And then he adds, 'But in his entering on that exile, it was holiness not hurt that was carrying him out of the Church of England.'[2]

★

What was he to do next? To seek priestly ordination was not a foregone conclusion, but in fact, in 1846 he went to Rome to prepare for priestly ordination and also to discern what kind of priestly life would be best for him. Following a suggestion by Nicholas Wiseman, who was now a bishop back in England and who in 1850 would be appointed the first Archbishop of Westminster, he decided eventually to join the Oratory of St Philip Neri whose boots, he had said, he would be prepared to black in heaven. It is easy to see what attracted him. Oratorians are diocesan priests, but they live in community. Their way of life could be seen as reflecting the kind of life with which Newman was familiar as an Oxford don, when the fellows, the senior members of the colleges, were unmarried and many of them were clergymen. And once he had made his decision, he was invited to adapt the Oratorian Rule for England. He went on to establish Oratories in Birmingham and London. But his troubles were far from over.

The English Catholic community at the time was small and lacking in self-confidence. It did not know what to do with the gifted man who had joined them. At various times in the coming years, Newman was invited to undertake projects – for example, to found a Catholic University in Dublin, to oversee a new translation of the Bible and to edit a distinguished, but at times controversial, Catholic periodical, called *The Rambler*. Newman accepted these invitations, but in each case he was not given the support or the resources to fulfil what was asked of him. They were difficult times. We will be noticing them again later. Time and again Newman felt frustrated. In a

2 Sheridan Gilley, *Newman and His Age* (London: Darton, Longman & Todd, 1990), p. 222.

lengthy entry in his journal in 1863, which was the darkest period of his life, he remarked, 'Since I have been a Catholic, I seem to myself to have had nothing but failure, personally' (*A.W.* p. 255).

Throughout these long, early Catholic years from 1845 to 1863, when Newman seemed to himself always to be failing, he also had to live with the knowledge that Protestant England thought him dishonest. No honest man of Newman's intelligence and distinction, it was believed, could conceivably have become a Catholic in good faith. There were suspicions, rumours and gossip that, perhaps for years before his formal reception, he had been a Catholic already, under cover within the Church of England, secretly and deceitfully making converts for Rome. Was he a fool or a liar?

Then, at the beginning of 1864, there was a sea change. Charles Kingsley, an Anglican priest, the Professor of Modern History at Cambridge University and a novelist, commented in passing in a book review for *Macmillan's Magazine* that 'Truth, for its own sake, had never been a virtue with the Roman clergy. Father Newman informs us that it need not, and on the whole ought not to be.' It was the kind of gratuitous slur that had become common. Indeed, when Newman wrote to the publisher, Alexander Macmillan, he received a courteous reply, but one in which Macmillan also observed of Kingsley's words: 'I have read the passage, and I will confess to you plainly that I did not even think at the time that you or any of your communion would think it unjust' (*L.D.* xxi, p. 12, n. 1 [363]).

Here was the common prejudice, expressed plainly and publicly. After the exchange of some letters with Kingsley that failed to resolve the matter, Newman set himself to write what became his most famous book, his *Apologia pro Vita Sua*. It was not an autobiography, but rather an account of his conversion to Rome, to vindicate his behaviour and to illustrate, whether people agreed with his position or not, that at least he had behaved honestly. The book was an overwhelming success and proved to be a turning point. Because Newman spoke so warmly of his old friends – many of whom had been out of contact with him for almost twenty years – it led to the healing of past hurts and the renewal of old and valued friendships. That earlier painful parting from friends began to be overcome.

But the difficult times were not all over. As there had been Anglicans who had doubted his integrity as one of them in times past, so there were Catholics who doubted the quality of his Catholicism now. His fellow convert, Henry Edward Manning, for example, who, though never especially close to Newman, had been his friend and who in 1865 was to become the Archbishop of Westminster and ten years later a cardinal, became as a Catholic fiercely ultramontane, that is to say, he identified being Catholic as being Roman. And he saw Newman as different. Manning was to say of him, 'I see much danger of an English Catholicism, of which Newman is the highest type.'[3] Newman, however, detected no difficulty in being both English and Catholic. In controversy with Gladstone in 1875 he would state plainly, 'I see no inconsistency in my being a good Catholic and a good Englishman' (*Diff.* ii, p. 77). And where that combination could be detected most clearly was perhaps in Newman's continued commitment to a middle way. The *via media* may have collapsed as an ecclesiology, but it had not disappeared altogether.

★

When Newman was made a cardinal in 1879, he made a speech that has become famous. He spoke against liberalism in religion, 'the doctrine that there is no positive truth . . . but that one creed is as good as another'. He declared that he had been

---

3 David Newsome, *The Convert Cardinals* (London: John Murray., 1993), p. 257.

opposed to such a view for thirty, forty, fifty years.[4] His words have at times been understood simplistically, especially by those of a more conservative temper who have wanted to claim Newman as one of their own. Newman, they like to declare, was 'against the liberals'. But the truth is far more subtle and interesting. He was responding to circumstances. That does not mean he was merely being subjective, but that he was reacting to the situation confronting him.

In his *Apologia*, Newman described dogma as 'the fundamental principle' of his religion (*Apo*. p. 49 [54]). As an Anglican, he had felt the need to champion it vigorously. He had opposed those who had come to regard creeds, in his words, as 'fetters on souls' (*P.S.* ii, p. 261), and those who dismissed the great Trinitarian and Christological controversies of the early Christian centuries as 'the strict and technical niceties of doctrine' (*P.S.* ii, pp,166–7). As an Anglican he had been ever vigilant in this cause.

And vigilant he remained as a Catholic, but his target in these later years was not other Christians, but infidelity. In a sermon in 1873 he spoke about a future when people in Great Britain would no longer believe. 'Christianity', he observed, 'has never yet had experience of a world simply irreligious.'[5] His awareness of what was to come had already been the spur for a plan that had failed, namely to establish an Oratory in Oxford.[6] He would not have gone to crusade against the established Church, as Pusey feared, but to act as a safeguard against infidelity for the young Catholics who might study there (see *L.D.* xxi, pp. 322–3, 327). He remained opposed to liberalism in religion.

---

4 Wilfrid Ward, *The Life of John Henry Cardinal Newman* ii, (London: Longmans, Green, and Co.) p. 460.
5 J. H. Newman, *Catholic Sermons of Cardinal Newman*, edited at the Birmingham Oratory (London: Burns & Oates, 1957), p. 121.
6 See chapter 7, p. 94.

However, as a Catholic among Catholics, he found that circumstances were very different from his experience as an Anglican. Among Catholics, dogma was not in danger; it was in the ascendant. But in the ascendant with it in certain quarters was a harsh, narrow, aggressive, dogmatising spirit intolerant of alternatives to its own viewpoint. It liked to elevate its own opinions into matters of faith. It had no time for schools of theology. Some of those who backed this way of thinking – such as Manning, the future cardinal; Frederick Faber, the Superior of the Brompton Oratory; and W. G. Ward – were men of real influence.

In the thick of writing his *Apologia* in 1864, there was an exchange of letters between Newman and Sir John (later Lord) Acton. In one of them Newman wrote, 'It seems impossible that active and sensible men can remain still under the dull tyranny of Manning and Ward' (*L.D.* xxi, p. 84). When Acton then encouraged Newman to tackle the crucial controversial issue of the Church's truthfulness, not just his own, in his *Apologia*, Newman replied, 'You may be sure I shall go as far as ever I can' (*L.D.* xxi, p. 94 [368]). As a Catholic he championed freedom in theology, because he was aware of the threat posed by dogmatic fundamentalism.

From this perspective, in the way he viewed the relationship between dogma and theology, we may perhaps detect in Newman's instinct for moderation another version of the middle way. He was arguing again for a *via media*, no longer now between two ecclesiological traditions, Protestant and Roman, but still between error and excess. He defended Church teaching, but was critical of Catholics who took matters to extremes and created unnecessary burdens for others. This approach is plainly evident in two of the major controversies in which he became involved, with Pusey in 1866 and then with Gladstone in 1874.

It is not necessary to explore the controversies themselves. Any biography of Newman will give the background. But what is noteworthy here is the way, in both cases – debating Marian doctrine and devotion with Pusey, and papal authority and infallibility with Gladstone – Newman was drawn in, not only in order to correct the mistakes and misconceptions that he felt Pusey and Gladstone had made, but also to temper the excesses of some Catholics. He was following a middle way. Writing to Pusey about Mary, he distanced himself from W. G. Ward and Frederick Faber and observed dryly in passing, 'I put aside the Archbishop, of course, because of his office' (*Diff.* ii, p. 22). And he explained that he wrote 'to avow plainly what I do and what I do not hold about the Blessed Virgin, that others may know, did they come to stand where I stand, what they would and what they would not, be bound to hold concerning her' (*Diff.* ii, p. 25).

When writing against Gladstone, there is a parallel disclaimer:

> I own to a deep feeling, that Catholics may in good measure thank themselves, and no one else, for having alienated from them so religious a mind [as Gladstone's]. There are those among us, as it must be confessed, who for years past have conducted themselves as if no responsibility attached to wild words and overbearing deeds; who have stated truths in the most paradoxical form, and stretched principles till they were close to snapping; and who at length, having done their best to set the house on fire, leave to others the task of putting out the flame (*Diff.* ii, pp. 176–7).

In both instances, he can be seen as navigating a course between error and excess.

Not everyone in Rome was best pleased with Newman's answer to Gladstone in particular. There was a feeling that he had not been as forthright as he should have been in defence of the papal position. In this instance, however, it was Manning who was prominent among those seeking to calm the potential Roman storm. He warned officials that their criticism of

Newman would do more harm than good, while Newman's own bishop, William Bernard Ullathorne, explained that Newman worked *ex abundantia concessionis*, ignoring lesser matters to secure the main argument.[7]

So it appears that Newman's instinct for moderation, for a kind of *via media*, his readiness to explore middle ground, was not something confined to his Anglican years. The focus may have shifted from his understanding of the Church to his approach in controversy, but the instinct remained and stood him in good stead. It revealed his gift for overcoming people's prejudices, for moving minds and touching hearts. Defending him to the Roman authorities, Ullathorne described Newman as having 'a tender and compassionate heart', and as exercising 'a great influence in conciliating to the faith minds in trouble'.[8] He was a wise, moderating influence.

After the death of Pope Pius IX in 1878, his successor, Leo XIII, who was an admirer of Newman's, decided to make him a cardinal. By that act Newman felt that the cloud, the suspicion that he was not truly a Catholic, had been lifted from him for ever. Some years later the Pope remarked, 'Il mio cardinale. It was not easy. They said he was too liberal, but I had determined to honour the Church in honouring Newman' (see *L.D.* xxix, p.xiii).

Newman lived for eleven more years and died peacefully in 1890.

★

Newman's life was long and varied, full of twists and turns, challenges and struggles. It was also a life lived faithfully. His peaceful deathbed was in marked contrast to the troubles and dark days he had had to endure. His experience may inspire

7 Cuthbert Butler, *The Life and Times of Bishop Ullathorne*, ii (London: Burns, Oates & Washbourne, 1926), p. 103.
8 ibid.

others whose lives, while apparently ordinary and undramatic, are never entirely free from anxiety. He can encourage them to remain steadfast and faithful.

Stephen Dessain, that prince of Newman scholars, used to say that Newman's devotion to the cause of revealed religion was what gave his life its unity.[9] And it was. What we believe is not of our making, but a gift from God. And hand in hand with that care for revealed religion was Newman's search for the Church, his desire to discover in its fullness the body of Christ, the community of faith, which recognises, receives and believes the revelation. It was what led him to pursue that pathway between error and excess.

Pope Paul VI, when beatifying Dominic Barberi in 1963, paused to speak of Newman's journey and described it as 'the most toilsome, but also the greatest, the most meaningful, the most conclusive, that human thought ever travelled . . . during the modern era, to arrive at the fullness of wisdom and of peace'.[10] Dessain once told me that with those words the Pope seemed to be beatifying Newman rather than Barberi.

These twin concerns, for revelation and for the Church, were also, of course, fundamental concerns of the Second Vatican Council which met between 1962 and 1965. Newman has been spoken of as the hidden father of that Council. So many of his preoccupations came into their own at that time: his opposition to clericalism and creeping infallibility, to unhistorical theology and exaggerated Mariology, and his advocacy of *ressourcement*, a return to Scripture and the Fathers, his championing of the Church as a communion and of the rightful place of the laity, his concern for unity, and his recognition of the necessary place of the Church in the world, responding to the needs and challenges it finds there. All these issues found

9 C. S. Dessain, *John Henry Newman* (Oxford: Oxford University Press, 1980), p. xii.
10 *The Divine Office* iii, p. 435*.

their place in the Council's work. Newman's voice was prophetic. All the same, he was rarely mentioned in the Council chamber. Nevertheless, if the Council was still in some sense Newman's Council, if the Council can still be seen in some way as Newman's hour, it was not so much because his ideas and thoughts had much immediate influence in the conciliar debates, but rather, as Professor Nicholas Lash has indicated, 'because during the Council the Catholic Church "caught up" with Newman'.[11] He was a pioneer, leading the way.

And underpinning these concerns were two others that are noteworthy. First, there was Newman's own faith in God, that initial conversion that had made its mark on him when he was fifteen. He had become convinced then of the existence of God in a way that was so profound that, he was to say, were he to doubt everything else, the two realities he could never doubt would be his own existence and that of his Creator (see *Apo*. p. 4 [17–18]). It fixed in him a profound sense of the relationship between the visible and the invisible worlds.

And second, this account of Newman has spoken principally of what he did, the events of his life. But underlying his behaviour there was also a pastoral motive. He is regarded as one of the great minds of the Christian Church. Erich Przywara, the German Jesuit scholar who died in 1972 but whose health had been damaged long before by his courageous resistance to National Socialism in Germany, linked Newman with Augustine and Aquinas. Przywara once observed, 'What St Augustine was for the ancient world, that St Thomas Aquinas was for the Middle Ages, and that Newman must be held to be in relation to the world of today.'[12] And yet Newman was never absorbed exclusively by

11 Nicholas Lash, 'Newman and Vatican II', *New Blackfriars* 92 (March 2011), p. 246.
12 See Louis Bouyer, *Newman: his Life and Spirituality* (London: Burns & Oates, 1958), p. 175.

ideas. Whether it was the students he taught, the congregations to which he preached, the parishes he served or the books he wrote, he was always concerned for people. He had no desire, he once declared, to overcome their reason without touching their hearts (see *G.A.* p. 425 [273]).

2

All that is, seen and unseen[1]

When people think about Newman, they tend to think immediately about his ideas, the contribution he has made to Christian thought. As the case may be, they are drawn by the account he gave of the relationship between faith and reason, they explore further his understanding of the development of Christian doctrine, they are inspired by his writings on conscience and they are attracted by the balanced way he handled controversy. So impressive and far ranging has Newman's contribution been that there have been those who, because his cause for beatification and canonisation seemed to be taking so long, would have preferred to bypass that process altogether and simply have him declared a Doctor of the Church. But the Church believes that someone who is recognised as one of its Doctors is not simply someone who has a brilliant intellect, someone whose ideas have been of benefit to the Church, however great that benefit may have been. The Church holds further that, when someone is acclaimed as a Doctor of the Church, there ought to be congruence between the ideas and the person. What the person says and who the person is need to be in tune.

That is not to say that saints are perfect, that they always practise exactly what they preach. Of course not. They, too,

1 Some of the material in this chapter, used with permission, is adapted from an article of mine in *Louvain Studies* (autumn, winter 2011), pp. 410–18.

make mistakes and sin. How comforting to hear Pope Benedict XVI declare at one of his Wednesday audiences in 2007 that 'the saints have not "fallen from Heaven". They are people like us, who also have complicated problems. Holiness does not consist in never having erred or sinned.'[2] Newman once said something similar about one of his heroes: St Cyril of Alexandria, who could be a ruthless operator. He did not feel obliged to defend everything Cyril had done. As he remarked, 'It does not answer to call whity-brown, white' (*H.S.* ii, p. 342). But when someone is held up as a great teacher, when someone is given the status of a Doctor of the Church, there ought to be a perceptible harmony between that person's life and their teaching. Those who are being declared Doctors of the Church are not being acclaimed for their ideas and their learning alone; their canonisation, as their beatification, means that they are being recognised as models who can be followed.

When Newman, therefore, was beatified by Pope Benedict, it was the man himself who was being acknowledged. That did not imply that he was perfect. He could, for example, be over-sensitive and angry, especially under pressure. But he was being recognised as a man of deep faith and steadfast fidelity through-out a long and often demanding life. Beatified, Newman, as we remarked earlier, was being held up as a witness to holiness, especially for the Church in Britain. His self-deprecating humour, his honesty and passion for truthfulness, illustrated by his *Apologia pro Vita Sua*, his pastoral sensitivity to those in need, and his gift for weighing up controversial arguments wisely may not be exclusively British qualities, but they commend themselves to the British character. Canonisation, however, is recognising something further, a depth of intimacy with God that goes beyond national character. So, as we begin to explore the source of Newman's holiness, we can start in the

2 See *L'Osservatore Romano*, Weekly Edition in English, 7 February 2007, p. 11.

most obvious place: by returning to his first experience of conversion.

★

In 1816, when he was only fifteen years old, Newman fell ill and remained at school throughout the long summer holiday. That was the time, as we have noticed, when he experienced what has come to be regarded as his first conversion. It had an evangelical flavour, although it was not a typically intense and subjective evangelical conversion. All the same, Newman came to believe in the doctrine of final perseverance and that he was 'elected to eternal glory' (*Apo.* pp. 4 [17]).

Elements of this experience faded before long. But something endured. In his *Apologia pro Vita Sua*, written many years later, in 1864, Newman described what had happened to him. He spoke of the experience as confirming his earlier childish mistrust of material phenomena, and then, in those words that have become famous, he declared how he came to rest 'in the thought of two and two only absolute and luminously self-evident beings, myself and my Creator' (*Apo.* p. 4 [17–18]). He was saying, in other words, that, were he to doubt everything else, what he could not doubt was his own existence and the existence of God. He was affirming something about the way he understood reality. That account of reality as a relationship between himself and God, between what is seen and what is unseen, between the visible and the invisible worlds, was absolutely fundamental for Newman. It shaped and conditioned his life ever after.

Newman was blessed with a formidably original mind. But originality can take various forms. There is one kind of originality that gathers in the evidence and examines it, and then arranges it in a way that has never been done before. Great theatre directors may do this. They take a classic text – a Shakespearean tragedy, for example – and then create a production that offers insights never realised before. They have not

added extra scenes, but they have drawn out themes and emphases that make it possible for those who come to the production
to see it with fresh eyes and appreciate it anew, in a way that has
never previously been done. In scholarly terms, you might think
of the way an outstanding graduate student or a researcher
reviews evidence and then presents it in a fresh way, in a way that
has never been imagined before. The researcher has put the old
pieces together but arranged them afresh. And virtually every
sentence ends with a reference to a footnote.

But there is another kind of originality, a kind that is less
tied to particular, detailed evidence. Every so often – though
rarely – people come along who think creatively and imagina-
tively. They see things differently. They have a capacity for
viewing a problem or an issue in a way that is not shaped
simply by a minute examination of the particular evidence.
Such people are not rearranging what has gone before.
Something more visionary is taking place. They have a gift for
looking with fresh eyes and seeing things whole. It seems to
me that Newman's originality was rather of this latter kind.

Samuel Taylor Coleridge once remarked in his table talk,
'Every man is born an Aristotelian, or a Platonist; I do not
think it possible that any one born an Aristotelian can become
a Platonist; and I am sure no born Platonist can change into an
Aristotelian.'[3] And the historian David Newsome has
suggested, that, if there is an exception to Coleridge's dictum,
it is Newman, 'born a Platonist', but through his education
'become an Aristotelian'.[4]

I am not sure that Newman is the unique exception that
Newsome claims, but the description seems to me to be sound.
He possessed a Platonist's capacity for seeing things whole, while

3 See H. J. Jackson (ed.), *Samuel Taylor Coleridge* (Oxford: Oxford
University Press, 1985), pp. 594–5.
4 David Newsome, *Two Classes of Men: Platonism and English Romantic
Thought* (London: John Murray., 1974), p. 72.

he also, as an Aristotelian, was able to analyse them in detail. But in identifying Newman's originality in particular as the kind that looks with fresh eyes and sees things whole, it is possible to discern something at a still deeper level, beyond a debate about the Platonist or Aristotelian approach. It is the freshness of view with Newman that is remarkable, that sense of reality as composed of the seen and the unseen, the visible and the invisible, woven together. When we look carefully, we can uncover clues.

★

In 1970, John Coulson produced a book entitled *Newman and the Common Tradition*. It was a study that explored, in particular, links in the works and thoughts of Newman and Coleridge: what was common to them was an awareness of language, of words, as not always arbitrary but as capable of sharing in the reality they expressed. Language could have a sacramental quality that opened up pathways into what was hidden.

Then, in an appendix, Coulson asked, 'How much of Coleridge had Newman read?'[5] In his old age, Newman had declared he had 'never read a line of Coleridge', a remark quoted by his biographer, Wilfrid Ward, as illustrating Newman's failing memory in his later years.[6] There is plenty of evidence to show that Newman had read Coleridge quite extensively. However, the point that is particularly interesting here is a comment in his 'Chronological Notes' in 1835, in which he wrote, 'During this spring (1835) I for the *first time* read parts of Coleridge's works; and I am surprised how much I thought mine, is to be found there.'[7] He was surprised how much he thought was his own. It suggests that Newman was

---

5 John Coulson, *Newman and the Common Tradition: A Study in the Language of Church and Society* (Oxford: Clarendon Press, 1970), pp. 254–5.
6 Wilfrid Ward, *The Life of John Henry Cardinal Newman* i, p. 58, n. 2.
7 See Anne Mozley, *Letters and Correspondence of John Henry Newman* ii (London: Longmans, Green, and Co, 1891), p. 39, n. 1.

not like some industrious graduate student who went around discovering precious nuggets in other people's work. No doubt he read extensively, especially when he was young, and used what he read in his own work. In later years, however, the pages in many of his books were uncut, which seems to indicate that he was not reading more generally but that he read to investigate what he was studying at that time, what held his attention. He read to test or reinforce something he already knew, something that resonated with a way of seeing things that had become natural to him.

In his *Apologia*, we can find another example. When referring to the influence on him of the Church of Alexandria, he wrote, 'The broad philosophy of Clement and Origen carried me away.' What touched him were passages in their writings that 'were based', as he put it, 'on the mystical or sacramental principle', passages that he understood to mean 'that the exterior world, physical and historical, was but the manifestation to our senses of realities greater than itself'. He explained that these 'portions of their teaching, magnificent in themselves, came like music to my inward ear, as if the response to ideas, which, with little external to encourage them, I had cherished so long' (*Apo.* pp. 26, 27 [36]). There it is again, the same notion. What Newman discovered in Clement and Origen, what appealed to him and made them so attractive, was not the novelty of their teaching, but a kind of recognition that registered within: what Newman heard he seemed already to know. What he already knew was the bond between all that is, seen and unseen.

The point can be made more generally as well. Although Newman read widely, it has often been noted that there are few footnotes in his work. Some will say that that was the custom of the time, and there may well be truth in that, but it may be the case that footnotes for Newman were nugatory. It was not that he refused to acknowledge his sources, pretending, so to speak, to pass off as his own what was really someone else's idea, but that what he had gained from others he often absorbed and used in ways that were distinctively and individually his. Direct quotations and references would almost have been misleading.

Sometimes you can find studies of some aspect of Newman's thought. These are excellent in their way: they take a scalpel to his work and examine it with the utmost care for detail. And yet there is something about the analysis – so minute, so detailed, so painstaking – that is ultimately unconvincing. It has examined the trees but failed somehow to see the wood. Analysis has obscured the vision. There is too little sensitivity to Newman's genius, his vision of reality in which what is seen and what is unseen, the visible and the invisible worlds, are woven together.

Consider what Newman had to say about miracles. The subject was topical when Newman was to be beatified, because there were those who argued that Jack Sullivan's cure, the healing of the crippling pain in his back, which had been attributed to his asking Newman to intercede for him and which had then been accepted as miraculous, making possible Newman's beatification, was in fact patient of a natural explanation. It may be unusual and rare, but may yet be considered as explicable by natural causes.[8]

It is important to proceed carefully. There is a danger that miracles become the last refuge of the *deus ex machina*, the god of the gaps: something extraordinary and exceptional happens, people seek an explanation, and, when they cannot find one, they conclude, 'God did it.' If that is the way miracles are to be understood, it would be better to abandon it. 'Gods of the gaps' have been thoroughly discredited.

Newman's view, however, was more subtle. He acknowledged that developments in science might reveal that events in the past that had been regarded as miraculous might not

8 See the discussion in John Cornwell, *Newman's Unquiet Grave: The Reluctant Saint* (London: Continuum, 2010), pp. 240–6.

actually be so. But he still believed in miracles, believed, that is to say, that God could act 'without the sequence of natural cause and effect', could intervene in his creation. He stated in his *Apologia*, 'That the Lawgiver always acts through His own laws, is an assumption of which I never saw a proof.' And he then noted that the possibility, therefore, 'of assigning a human cause for an event does not *ipso facto* prove that it is not miracu- lous' (*Apo.* p. 303 [266]). In other words, there is more to a miracle than what is humanly or naturally explicable. And so, shortly afterwards, he observed:

> Providences, or what are called *grazie*, though they do not rise to the order of miracles, yet, if they occur again and again in connexion with the same persons, institutions, or doctrines, may supply a cumulative evidence of the fact of a supernatural pres- ence in the quarter in which they are found (*Apo.* p. 304 [267]).

The key issue here is not miracles as such, but the awareness of the nature of reality that is implied: the Creator is present within creation and at times something occurs that is extraor- dinary and exceptional. Though not necessarily beyond human or natural explanation, it is nevertheless sufficiently extraordi- nary and sufficiently exceptional to alert us to that presence.

What Newman recognised in miracles, he also recognised elsewhere, of course. His view of miracles blended with his view of reality as sacramental, a conviction that lay at the heart of the Tractarian outlook. In his paper to the Oxford Symposium on Newman in 1966, Canon Donald Allchin reminded those present of a letter Newman had written to his sister, Jemima, in May 1828, after the death of their sister Mary in the January. Newman had been out for a ride to visit friends and was relieved to have got out of Oxford. The ride had done him good. All the same, his grief at Mary's death was still intense and painful. He mentioned 'the fresh leaves, the scents, the varied landscape'. But then he went on, 'Yet I never felt so intensely the transitory nature of this world as when most delighted with these country scenes', and he quoted two lines from the verse of a hymn by his friend, John Keble. The whole stanza reads:

> Every leaf in every nook,
> Every wave in every brook,
> Chanting with a solemn voice,
> Minds us of our better choice.[9]

'Chanting with a *solemn* voice, / minds us of our *better* choice' were the lines he quoted. There is something beyond the beauty that we see. And he remarked, 'I could hardly believe the lines were not my own and Keble had not taken them from me.' There it is again, the theme we have noticed before: Newman was touched by what seemed to him to be his own. Mary, he said, seemed to be 'embodied in every tree and hid behind every hill'. And he commented, 'What a veil and curtain this world of sense is! beautiful but still a veil' (*L.D.* ii, p. 69).

These lines of Keble's, unremarkable in themselves, were significant for the Tractarians more generally. They were also used by Edward Pusey in his lectures on *Types and Prophecies* eight years later. Although of no special merit in themselves, they nevertheless capture, as Donald Allchin observed, 'two central elements in the Tractarian vision of the world and of God'. The first is that '*everything* created shouts the glory of its Maker'; and the second that 'at the moment of recognising the utter transcendence of God we also experience his agonising nearness'.[10] Here was that vision of reality that Newman recognised, where the visible and the invisible worlds were woven

9 John Keble (1792–1866), 'The Nightingale'.
10 A. M. Allchin, 'The Theological Vision of the Oxford Movement', in John Coulson and A. M. Allchin (eds), *The Rediscovery of Newman* (London: Sheed & Ward/SPCK, 1967), pp. 53–4.

together as one. It might even be seen as reflected in his every-day life: Newman who had such a genius for friendship, but was said never to be less alone than when alone: *numquam minus solus quam cum solus.*

★

Holiness can take many forms. There are saints who give their lives for others, like Maximilian Kolbe; there are martyrs who are killed brutally; there are mystics, like Teresa of Avila and John of the Cross; teachers, like Augustine and Aquinas; and so many others who are models of holiness. Newman's witness to holiness can be seen in more ways than one. He was a teacher. He was also a pastor. He had a passion for the truth. He was diffident and self-deprecating. But he also embraced the paschal mystery throughout his long life, during which his hopes and plans were often thwarted and he suffered disappointment and frustration time after time.

But, besides all that, there was something else that was fundamental to him as a person – his perception of a truth about reality, about all that is, the intimate bond between what is seen and what is unseen – that dawned on him as a boy of fifteen and ever after shaped his life. It makes him an outstanding model of holiness for our world today, someone who can speak to us of God, to borrow Pope Paul VI's memorable phrase, as if he could 'see the invisible'.[11] That was Newman. That was the bedrock of his own spiritual life and the very heart of the witness to holiness he offers.

And that bond between what is seen and what is unseen he believed to be revealed in the Christ. It is necessary to be alert, to be on the watch.

11 Pope Paul VI, *Evangelii Nuntiandi*, n. 76.

3

Watching for Christ

Entering Harlem during his visit to the United States in 1979, Pope John Paul II cried out, 'We are an Easter people and "Alleluia" is our song.' His words lifted people's hearts.

It can be claimed, of course, that Christians are a people of every liturgical season. They are an incarnational people when they celebrate at Christmas the Word made flesh, the birth of Jesus as their brother and Saviour; a penitential people during Lent; a people of the cross during Holy Week; and, indeed, an Easter people during Eastertide; and then at Pentecost a people of the Spirit. But they can also claim that they are, in a very particular way, 'an Advent people, and "Maranatha, come, Lord Jesus" is their song'. Why? Because throughout our lives we need always to be looking to the past, to our roots in the birth and ministry, death and resurrection of the Christ. We should equally be looking to the future, living in expectation of his second coming, and in every moment of our lives be on the watch for his presence now in our midst, in the world, in society and in our own hearts. Advent is the season when that threefold perspective, which should be characteristic of the Christian disposition every day, is most clearly evident. It is the time when Christians are called most explicitly to be on the watch for Christ, in the past, in the future and in the present.

I mention this because it may be that Advent was in fact the season Newman valued most highly of all. Preaching in February 1843, he declared, 'This is the very definition of a Christian, – one who looks for Christ; not who looks for gain, or distinction, or power, or pleasure, or comfort, but who looks "for the Saviour, the Lord Jesus Christ"' (*S.D.* pp. 278–9). To watch for Christ, to be on the alert for his presence, is an essential feature of Advent, but it is also the essential feature of all Christian living. It was a key aspect of Newman's own spirituality. To be intimate with Christ is to be alert to his presence.

One way to explore Newman's desire to look for Christ can be found by considering in particular three of his sermons. They are all linked to the season of Advent or to Christmas. But before doing so, it may help to be clear about a truth close to Newman's heart.

★

People with only a smattering of knowledge about Newman tend at least to have heard of the distinction he made between notional and real assent in *A Grammar of Assent*. In brief, while notional assents tend to be intellectual and abstract, real assents are concrete and stir people to action. And as we have noticed already, Newman never wished to move people's minds without touching their hearts (see *G.A.* p. 425 [273]). His motto as a cardinal was 'Heart speaks to heart' – *Cor ad cor loquitur.*

But there is a question that can be asked. Was this a Catholic novelty, something that became significant for him after his conversion in 1845? After all, as an Anglican he had opposed both evangelicals and liberals who themselves laid great emphasis on the heart. Had he changed? Was he being inconsistent?

He was not. There was a crucial difference during his Anglican days between his position and the position adopted by the evangelicals and liberals he was criticising. From their distinct viewpoints, the teaching that mattered to them both was what touched the heart; what did not, they argued, could therefore be disregarded or ignored. The effect felt on the heart was what counted. That was the criterion for its significance. For evangelicals it was what moved the heart; what did not, they dismissed out of hand. For liberals it was what was personal and useful. For the Anglican Newman, however, a teaching's effect on the heart was not the criterion for its value; for him the criterion was that it was true. What was true, however, should never be merely a matter for the mind. Truth should move the heart also. As he stated in the first of these sermons we shall consider, a sermon which he called 'Unreal Words', 'we ought to have our hearts penetrated with the love of Christ and full of self-renunciation'. However, he went on, if they are not penetrated with that love and filled with such humility, then 'professing that they are does not make them so' (P.S. v, p. 39). That sentence is the pivot on which the whole sermon revolves. It is time to look at it more closely.

★

'Unreal Words'

When Newman published his sermons, he arranged them in a way that seemed appropriate to him in relation to the liturgical year, even though he may have preached them first of all at a different time. So, although he preached this sermon first on 2 June 1839, it is named as an Advent sermon. 'Unreal Words' (P.S. v, pp. 29–45) is a powerful piece, and it is not about what Christians profess or believe, or prayer, and so forth, but about their behaviour, the way they live. The crux of its message affirms that *how* Christians profess their convictions, *how* they believe, *how* they pray, *how* they treat people, *how* they speak, *how* they argue and *how* they teach must all be done sincerely, or, he adds, 'to use an expressive word, must be *real*' (P.S. v, p. 31). Their words must be real. And the basis for this assertion is to be found at the very beginning of the sermon, where Newman stated:

Before Christ came was the time of shadows; but when He came, He brought truth as well as grace; and as He who is the Truth has come to us, so does He in return require that we should be true and sincere in our dealings with Him (*P.S.* v, p. 29).

What a fascinating sentence that is.

Remember where we are, when this sermon was originally being preached. It was the beginning of June. The summer term at Oxford was coming to an end, and during the long vacation that year, 1839, Newman was about to return to reading at leisure the history of Monophysitism. It was while he was doing so, as he was to explain in his *Apologia*, 'that for the first time a doubt came upon me of the tenableness of Anglicanism' (*Apo.* p. 114 [108]). So when he was preaching this sermon that doubt had not yet struck him. Here was Newman at the height of his influence as an Anglican and as a leader of the Oxford Movement speaking of Christianity as carrying people from shadows into truth. He was anticipating what he would express many years later in the epitaph he composed for himself: *ex umbris et imaginibus in veritatem*, 'from shadows and images into the truth'. It is one of those touches that reflects the consistency of Newman's thinking as both an Anglican and a Catholic.

The target Newman was criticising was, therefore, insincerity; unreal or unsubstantial professions, as he called them; professions of faith that had not been taken to heart. He referred to such professions as 'edged tools' (*P.S.* v, p. 33). The image is not of the double-edged sword of the Letter to the Hebrews (4:12), but rather refers to the kind of instrument a sculptor uses to carve something beautiful, but which, in the hand of a child or someone inexperienced, can be dangerous and cause harm. Newman was criticising people who speak insincerely, pontificating on serious matters without expertise, so their words are unreal.

He gave a range of examples to illustrate what he meant by such words. He spoke of people in new company who are quick to make judgments, whether favourable or not, on those who as yet they hardly know; people with poor sight who try to decide questions of proportion or colour; people with no ear for music who nevertheless pass judgment on a piece they have heard; people who air their views on moral matters or politics or religion without troubling to be properly informed. He gave various other examples as well and concluded, 'They have no means of judging, no standard to measure by, – and they give judgment at random, saying yea or nay on very deep questions, according as their fancy is struck at the moment, or as some clever or specious argument happens to come across them . . . All this is to be unreal' (P.S. v, p. 36).

What he was encouraging was a way of speaking that corresponds to the way people feel. That is plain from something he said earlier, which is astonishing. He affirmed that 'a person who is really honest, is already perfect', and so such a person is rare indeed (P.S. v, p. 31). He also allowed that it 'takes a long time really to feel and understand things as they are; we learn to do so only gradually' (P.S. v, p. 43). Being honest, speaking truthfully and sincerely, so that words and feelings are in tune, does not come easily. It takes time.

And so he came to speak of religious emotions in particular. The deep mysteries of faith that should move people: the tragedy of sin, the wonder of the Lord's divinity and the atonement gained for the human race, the grace of baptism, these truths 'are so vast', Newman commented, 'that no one can realize them without very complicated and profound feelings'. People may recognise the importance and profundity of the teaching and that they should arouse deep feelings, but they cannot create the feelings simply by laying claim to them.

Then comes that pivotal sentence. Newman was emphatic: 'Let us never lose sight of two truths, – that we ought to have our hearts penetrated with the love of Christ and full of self-renunciation; but that if they be not, professing that they are does not make them so' (*P.S.* v, 38–9). Words alone, protestations, are not enough. Words become real when they are sincere and find a home in the heart.

Newman's reflection on unreal words was intended to encourage people to 'aim at meaning what [they] say, and saying what [they] mean', in the sense of 'knowing when [they] understand a truth, and when [they] do not'. They have to be genuine, honest, authentic. As people seek to move out of the shadows into the truth, they are attempting something that is not easy, namely, 'to learn that new language which Christ has brought [them]'. 'There are', Newman said, 'ten thousand ways of looking at this world, but only one right way . . . Aim at looking at it in God's way. Aim at seeing things as God sees them . . . All things that we see are but shadows to us and delusions, unless we enter into what they really mean' (*P.S.* v, pp. 44–5).

People have to learn to move *ex umbris et imaginibus in veritatem*, 'from the shadows into truth', into reality. That is the outlook by which they will become more sensitive to Christ. They will become alert, on the watch for his presence. We return to our starting point: 'the very definition of a Christian [is] one who looks for Christ'.

Newman was insistent, therefore, that people must be on the watch for Christ. They have to remove the barrier of unreality, of insincerity, and look for Christ prayerfully, in a spirit of detachment and filled with joy. These qualities of prayer, detachment and joy are marks of being truly Christian (see *S.D.* pp. 280–7). They alert people to look for Christ. That watchfulness is the essential mark, the foundation, according to Newman, of being a Christian (see *S.D.* p. 279).

There is another sermon, called simply 'Watching' (*P.S.* iv, pp. 319–33), in which Newman described his understanding of watchfulness.

'Watching'

Newman first preached this sermon on 3 December 1837, the first Sunday of Advent that year. There he stated the issue and put the question starkly: 'true Christians, whoever they are, watch . . . Now what is watching?' (*P.S.* iv, p. 322).

The answer that he gave is all the more engaging because, in a different sermon, he gave the same reply virtually word for word. This other sermon, called, 'Waiting for Christ', is one of a series he was to preach nineteen years later, in 1856 when he was Rector of the Catholic University he had founded in Dublin. Here again is another indication of the link between the Anglican and Catholic Newman. He framed his answer by asking a series of questions:

> Do you know the feeling in matters of this life, of expecting a friend, expecting him to come, and he delays? Do you know what it is to be in unpleasant company, and to wish for the time to pass away, and the hour strike when you may be at liberty? Do you know what it is to be in anxiety lest something should happen which may happen or may not, or to be in suspense about some important event, which makes your heart beat when you are reminded of it, and of which you think the first thing in the morning? Do you know what it is to have a friend in a distant country, to expect news of him, and to wonder from day to day what he is now doing, and whether he is well? Do you know what it is so to live upon a person who is present with you, that your eyes follow his, that you read his soul, that you see all its changes in his countenance, that you anticipate his wishes, that you smile in his smile, and are sad in his sadness, and are downcast when he is vexed, and rejoice in his successes? To watch for Christ is a feeling such as all these; as far as feelings of this world are fit to shadow out those of another (*P.S.* iv, pp. 322–3; *O.S.* pp. 35–6).

What makes the passage powerful is the personal quality of the questions, the appeal to experience. Who has not waited anxiously for a friend whose arrival has been delayed? Which of us has not been cornered somewhere by a bore, in a meeting or at a party, and longed to get away? Which of us has not felt weighed down with worry about some impending event of great importance – perhaps something personal or something professional, or maybe political – that floods our waking moments, wondering whether it is going to turn out badly or well? Who has not felt concern for a sick friend, especially someone who is far away whom we cannot visit, and wondered how they are? (When he first wrote those words in 1837, Newman must almost certainly have been recalling his own anxiety during the illness of his friend, Hurrell Froude, who had died from tuberculosis the previous year.) Or who has not been in the company of someone they love and been sensitive to their moods and feelings, calm or cheerful, or downhearted? The anxiety, worry or concern, as well as the pleasure at a friend's happiness or success, prompt watchfulness, make people alert to what is happening and to what may happen next.

The very definition of a Christian is one who looks for Christ, gazing into the past, discerning his presence in the mysteries of faith, contemplating the future and wondering when he will come again, but attentive also to the present moment, on the watch for his presence now. For Newman, being on the watch was an integral aspect of Christian living.

'Christ Hidden from the World'

On Christmas Day that same year, 1837, Newman preached a sermon he called 'Christ Hidden from the World' (*P.S.* iv, pp. 238–52). He began simply, speaking in a way that may seem conventionally pious, referring to Jesus as not born into wealth and grandeur, which would have made him noticeable, but instead being born into poverty and even contempt. He referred next to the journey to Bethlehem, to there being no room in the inn and to the child being born in a stable and laid in a manger. He continued, 'That little babe, so born, so placed, is none other than the Creator of heaven and earth, the Eternal Son of God' (*P.S.* iv, p. 241). Here is the conventional teaching: God was made man, the Word became flesh.

He turned next to Jesus' public ministry and the fact that this began thirty years later. And when it did, people were astonished by him. Those close to him, even some of his own family, thought he was 'beside Himself' (Mark 3:21). They wondered whether he was going mad. Why did they think that?

Here the mood of the sermon changes, with one of those imaginative shifts typical of Newman. He explained the disciples' failure to recognise him. Familiarity had bred, if not contempt, at least a kind of blindness. Their view of him was blinkered:

> They had lived so long with Him, and yet did not know Him; did not understand what He was. They saw nothing to mark a difference between Him and them. He was dressed as others, He ate and drank as others, He came in and went out, and spoke, and walked, and slept, as others. He was in all respects a man, except that He did not sin, and this great difference the many would not detect, because none of us understands those who are much better than himself: so that Christ, the sinless Son of God, might be living close to us, and we not discover it.

Then at once Newman underlined this final point: 'I say that Christ, the sinless Son of God, might be living now as our next door neighbour, and perhaps we not find it out' (*P.S.* iv, p. 242).

That idea triggered a passage in which he spoke about the large number of people who are respectable, decent and outwardly correct, although they may have no particular religious convictions. His description, of course, is of his time, but it can easily be translated and transferred to the present day. And then there are others, he went on to notice, apparently indistinguishable from this first set, who nevertheless are very different because what they do, they do in secret, they 'look about the same, to common eyes, because true religion is a hidden life in the heart; and', he added, 'though it cannot exist without deeds, yet these are for the most part secret deeds, secret charities, secret prayers, secret self-denials, secret struggles, secret victories' (P.S. iv, p. 243). Christ is still present on earth in holy men and women. But is he recognised within them?

Newman continued by speaking of Christ's presence through the presence of the Spirit (see P.S. iv, p. 249), and of his presence as well through his body, the Church, in spite of it being 'a body of humiliation, almost provoking insult and profaneness, when men do not live by faith' (P.S. iv, p. 250). The Church is an earthen vessel, a vessel of clay. Christ is present in children so that those who receive them receive him (Matthew 18:5); and he is present in those who are hungry and thirsty, the strangers and those who are naked, sick and imprisoned, for what we do to them, we do to him (Matthew 25:35–40); and he is present in the sacraments.

Newman ended by inviting people to pray that the eyes of their understanding may be enlightened, so that 'the spiritual heart may approach Him, possess Him, see Him, even upon earth' (P.S. iv, pp. 250–2).

These three sermons may be read, therefore, as offering a guide, helping people to be on the watch for Christ. Words that are sincere, that are real, will help to make people alert, so that they become sensitive to Christ's presence, which they may discover in many places: in the Church, in spite of its frailty; in the sacraments; in their friends and others whom they meet; and in those in need. Moreover, that presence summons people, calls to them, and it does so more than once.

★

Some years ago, shortly before a friend of mine died, one of his daughters happened to come across a passage from Newman's writings that afterwards she read at his Requiem Mass. The words come from the sermon 'Divine Calls' which Newman first preached on 27 October 1839 and in which he reminded his congregation:

> For in truth we are not called once only, but many times; all through our life Christ is calling us. He called us first in Baptism; but afterwards also; whether we obey his voice or not, He graciously calls us still. If we fall from our Baptism, He call us to repent; if we are striving to fulfil our calling, He calls us on from grace to grace, and from holiness to holiness, while life is given us (*P.S.* viii, p. 23).

These words brought comfort to my friend's family and others who were present because they seemed in a way to correspond to his experience of faith throughout his life. He had been called when he was baptised, called when he married, called as the father of a family and as a businessman. Throughout that time, however, although he was a practising Catholic, his faith had not been especially significant for him. Then he was called again, challenged by the decision of his other daughter to change her career from banking to nursing, a decision he did not welcome. But then he was called again: by reflecting on her decision he was led to assess his own priorities, which led in turn to a deepening and renewal of his faith and his service to the Church. And he was called afresh in his final illness and at the time of his dying. He was indeed called not once, but many times. These words, as I say, brought comfort to the family because they captured a truth about the man who had died. But they are applicable to many people, and they are also applicable to Newman.

Newman did not parade himself in his sermons, but now and then something more personal seemed to break through. That could be true here. A little later, he explained:

> I am not speaking of cases when people change their position, their place in society, their pursuit, and the like; I am supposing them to remain pretty much the same as before in outward circumstances; but I say that many a man is conscious to himself of having undergone inwardly great changes of view as to what truth is and what happiness (*P.S.* viii, p. 26).

Consider again those last words: he was not speaking of cases when people change their position or place in society; they remain where they were, but they become conscious to themselves of having undergone great changes of view as to what truth is and what happiness is. Whereas the sermon 'Unreal Words', as we noticed, was preached just before the long summer holiday in 1839, this one came just afterwards, in the October of that year, when Newman had found himself wondering whether, when he championed the *via media* and looked in the mirror, he saw himself as a Monophysite. He had not changed his position or place in society at that time; he remained where he was. But had some great inward change taken place?

Writing that sermon, had Newman been reflecting on events in his own life that could be seen as divine calls? When he spoke, had he been prompted by recalling the early illnesses that had influenced him? In 1816, when ill health had forced him to remain at school, there had been that initial powerful experience of conversion; in late 1827 and early 1828, when he had been unwell again and then his sister Mary had died, illness and bereavement had called him on from contentment with intellectual excellence to something deeper; and then in Sicily in 1833, though unwell for a third time, he had had a sense that God still had a work for him to do, a work that bore fruit in the Oxford Movement: 'Lead, kindly light, Lead Thou me on' (*V.V.* p. 156).

Whether consciously or not, this sermon can seem to have been influenced to some degree by those calls. At the same time, it may be seen with hindsight as prophetic, pointing as well to the call that would lead him in the years immediately after he had preached it, not, after all, to remain where he was, but to turn away from the Church of England and embrace communion with Rome. That call would hold him steadfast through the many dark and desolate years that would follow that decision, and later would bring him peace in old age when he was made a cardinal.

Throughout his life, Newman never forgot to be faithful himself to the path that he urged others to follow, speaking real words, remaining watchful and keeping his heart 'penetrated with the love of Christ' (*P.S.* v, p. 39).

4

Life in Christ

If the very definition of a Christian is one who looks for Christ, it is natural to ask who was the Christ for whom Newman looked. Who did he say Jesus was?

At Christmas in 1889, which was to be Newman's last, the appointed preacher failed to arrive. The old cardinal, it is said, felt so fit that he was ready to take his place and was disappointed when one of the other priests from the community forestalled him. He was going to preach on growing disbelief in the divinity of Christ.[1]

That readiness to preach about Christ can be seen as evidence of Newman's own heart being penetrated with love for Christ. He had been a priest for so long – virtually twenty years as an Anglican, almost forty-three as a Catholic – that is hardly surprising. And it was, of course, a Christmas sermon so the subject suggested itself naturally enough. All the same, his chosen theme – growing disbelief in the divinity of Christ – may cause difficulties for some. They wonder whether it suggests an imbalance in his understanding of Christ.

Long ago, the German-American theologian, Hilda Graef, observed, 'In his reaction against the purely human Christ of rationalism [Newman] often preaches a Christ whose divinity is emphasized to such a degree as to make him almost

---

1 See Meriol Trevor, *Newman: Light in Winter* (London: Macmillan & Co., 1962), p. 640.

unapproachable.'[2] Was that what was happening again on that Christmas Day in 1889?

Gabriel Daly, the distinguished Irish Augustinian, perhaps captured the problem most succinctly, when he adopted Newman's later terminology from *A Grammar of Assent* and remarked that, while he always covers the orthodox bases, Newman's Christ is 'really divine and notionally human'. Shortly afterwards he concluded that 'it is hard to deny that Newman shared in the functional monophysitism of traditional orthodoxy'.[3] That orthodox care for Christ's divinity has indeed often slipped more generally into functional mono-physitism – the failure, in other words, to take Christ's human-ity seriously enough and see him as a recognisable human being. Was that really true of Newman?

We have recognised already that Newman regarded himself as an occasional writer, not in the sense of someone who only wrote occasionally, but because, as we have seen, almost invari-ably he wrote in response to a special need or an occasion. Given the temper of his times to underestimate the divinity of Christ, and given his instinct for apologetic writing, respond-ing to need and occasion, and given, too, the fact that, when he wrote about Christ, he generally did so in the context of his study of the Fathers, and especially of the Arian controversy in the fourth century, a teaching judged heretical because it had called Christ's divinity into question, it is hardly surprising that what he wrote was weighted towards highlighting and safe-guarding that divinity. This is not the place to explore the specific details of that controversy or to debate the balance of

2 Hilda Graef, *God and Myself: The Spirituality of John Henry Newman* (London: The Catholic Book Club, 1967), pp. 51–2.
3 Gabriel Daly, review of Roderick Strange, *Newman and the Gospel of Christ* (Oxford: Oxford University Press, 1981), in *Journal of Ecclesiastical History*, 35 (1984), pp. 289–90.

Newman's understanding of Christ.[4] All the same, there is one extended piece of writing about Christ that Newman left. It is a set of four unpublished sermons that he preached between 24 April and 16 May 1836.[5]

★

These four sermons present, unsurprisingly, a straightforward, traditional and balanced account of orthodox Christian teaching on the mystery of the incarnation. When considering such matters, Newman had no desire to be original. Christians believe that the Christ is divine, is human and is one – that is to say, in him the divine and human natures are united perfectly without being compromised. That is the teaching these sermons present. When people have failed to embrace the mystery, they have tended to be mistaken in one of three ways: either they have acknowledged Jesus as truly divine but only

4 Those wishing to explore further may consider Strange, *Newman and the Gospel of Christ*, especially pp. 47–95; Gabriel Daly's review, see above, n. 3; and Roderick Strange, 'Newman and the Mystery of Christ', in Ian Ker and Alan G. Hill (eds), *Newman after a Hundred Years* (Oxford: Clarendon Press, 1990), pp. 323–36.

5 Newman's unpublished sermons have now been published in five volumes, and these sermons on Christ appear in Francis J. McGrath (ed.), *John Henry Newman: Sermons 1824–1843*, iv (Oxford: Clarendon Press, 2011), pp. 206–23. The original manuscripts are in the archive of the Birmingham Oratory, as MS. Sermons nos 405–408. Some of the text of Sermons 405 and 406 was combined by Newman to form the sermon he published as 'Christ, the Son of God Made Man' (*P.S.* vi, pp. 53–68), but not in their entirety. For some reason, although the unpublished no 406 has been printed, no 405 has been omitted. Its text was seen as included in the published sermon. Some parts of it have, however, been omitted. In 1978, Fr Gregory Winterton, who was the Provost of the Oratory at the time, sent me photocopies of these sermons, which I had already copied for my own research. Quotations will come from the now published volumes, except the references to Ms. Sermon no 405, which will be taken from the manuscript copy.

apparently human; or as an inspiringly holy man, perhaps in fact the greatest saint who has ever lived, without actually being divine; or as someone in whom the human and the divine were both realised, but without being truly united. Those aware of early controversies in the Church – Docetist, Arian, Apollinarian, Monophysite, Nestorian – will recognise the patristic undertones.

All these sermons of Newman's reflected on the incarnate Christ, God made man, but the emphasis shifted as the series continued. In the first one, after setting out those three ways in which people tend to approach the mystery mistakenly, which he indicated existed in his own day (and which, we might add, exist still in ours), he concluded, 'None of the three [positions] took in the true notion of the *Christ*, the one Christ, at once God and man.'[6] So, at the start, he emphasised Christ as one. Then he moved on to affirm Christ as divine:

> The course of error then at the present day seems to be this – first to forget that our Lord is the Son of God in His *divine* nature – to speak of Him vaguely as God, which most surely He is, but vaguely, not as being what He is also – God from God – light from light – very God from very God.[7]

Newman then considered the way Christ's humanity is related to his divinity. He was intent on presenting the orthodox teaching of the Council of Chalcedon that Christ is one divine Person in two natures: the divine and the human. He stated, for example, that when Christ assumed our human nature, he took our flesh:

6 Ms. Sermon no 405, p. 5.
7 Ms. Sermon no 406, in *John Henry Newman: Sermons 1824–1843*, iv, p. 207.

into His own previous personality <what He was before>[8] –
so that He is not, strictly speaking, an individual man as other
men, but He is set before us as acting in two natures, God
acting as God and man.

The affirmation that Jesus shares perfectly our human nature,
while denying that he is a human person, in our ordinary use
of the word, but associating his human nature with his previous – in other words, his divine personality – is the notion that
has drawn the criticism we noticed earlier. Newman, however,
went on to explain:

> When our Lord took human flesh, He still remained divine
> and all perfect, as He had been from eternity – He did not
> subject His divine mind to human nature, but He took human
> nature into Himself, so that it should be entirely subordinate to
> His Godhead . . . but though His divine nature was thus sover-
> eign and supreme when He became incarnate, yet the human
> nature which He assumed was not kept at a distance from Him
> (so to speak) or put on as a mere garment or entered as a mere
> tabernacle, but really taken into the closest and most intimate
> union with Him.[9]

Intimacy is affirmed, but without a human subject. In a
published sermon, composed at this time and which made use
of these unpublished sermons, he even declared that:

> though He [Christ] was in nature perfect man, He was not man
> in exactly the same sense in which any one of us is a man.
> Though man, He was not, strictly speaking, *a* man; . . . He was
> man because He had our human nature wholly and perfectly,
> but His Person is not human like ours, but divine (*P.S.* vi, p. 62).

8 The phrase in angled brackets was a clarification added by Newman.
9 ibid., no. 406, p. 208.

What Newman needed here, but lacked, was the distinction that the former Archbishop of Canterbury, Rowan Williams, began to explore most helpfully many years ago: the distinction between person and personality. They are not identical. The Godhead of Jesus, the divine Person, may be located, Williams argued, at a level deeper than that of personality. And so, to affirm that the Second Person of the Trinity, the divine Word, assumed human nature does not entail denying to that human nature what we are now able to understand human personality to be.[10] Newman did not have that distinction, so to speak, at his disposal. All the same, that was plainly what he was wanting to affirm. In another published sermon, 'The Incarnate Son, a Sufferer and Sacrifice', which he preached on Good Friday in that very year, 1836, when he delivered these unpublished sermons, he described Christ's manhood as 'truly and personally His' (*P.S.* vi. p. 73), and some years later, as a Catholic in 1850, he was to refer to the 'two *subjects* of the union, of the divinity and of the manhood' (*Mix.* p. 348).

In the third of these sermons Newman focused on Christ as human. He began by declaring, 'When our Blessed Lord, the Son of God became man, He took on Him our created nature so perfectly that He was as much man as if He had ceased to be God.' It was the kind of formula he used frequently. In that Good Friday sermon he declared that the Son of God:

> was truly God, but He became as truly man. He became man, yet not so as to cease in any respect being what he was before. He added a new nature to Himself, yet so intimately, that it was *as if* he had actually left His former self, which He did not (*P.S.* vi, pp. 71–2).

10 See Rowan Williams, ' "Person" and "Personality" in Christology', *Downside Review* xciv (October 1976), pp. 253–60.

Some weeks later, he observed that the Eternal Word was 'as entirely man as if He had ceased to be God, as fully God as if He had never become man, as fully both at once as He was in being at all' (*P.S.* vi, p. 66). And in one of his notes for the translation he made of the Athanasian Treatises, he said the same: '[Christ] is as simply God as if He were not man, as simply man as if He were not God' (*Ath.* ii. p. 326). And then in the unpublished sermon he continued immediately, 'He was as entirely man with the substance of body and soul, with all the thoughts, feelings, and powers of man (sin excepted) as if He were nothing besides, as if, keeping His personality, He had changed His nature.'[11]

The major stumbling-block for this understanding of Christ, influenced significantly by St Athanasius and the Alexandrian School which Newman so admired, is whether it allows Christ genuine human experience. Or does the divine nature of the Christ so swamp the human as to compromise the authenticity of that experience? Did the Alexandrians, in their care for the unity of the Christ, fail to recognise his human soul? Is the human soul of the Christ overwhelmed by the divine Word?

In his controversy with the Arians, Athanasius famously makes no clear reference to Christ's human soul. It would have been a telling point against their claim that the Christ was a middle being of unique character, wondrous but not truly divine, human but lacking a human soul. To affirm the human soul would have allowed Athanasius to affirm a human subject, especially for Jesus' experience of weakness, tiredness, hunger, fear and so on. There have been lengthy scholarly debates on the subject. It need not detain us further here. What we can notice is the clarity with which Newman affirmed that Christ is fully human and so has a soul. For him, to deny a human

---

11 Ms. Sermon no 407, *John Henry Newman: Sermons 1824–1843*, iv, p. 214.

soul to Christ is to fall into error, 'the error, I mean, of forget-
ting or denying that our Lord Himself had a human soul'.[12] He
continued by referring rather simply to various Scripture
passages that speak of Christ's soul, such as the Marcan text,
'*My soul* is exceedingly sorrowful unto death' (Mark 14:34). At
this point in his text he also scribbled a note in pencil that
reads, 'Here insert about his sorrowing, fearing, etc.', which is,
of course, the very point that scholars have found wanting in
the approach of Athanasius.[13]

What Newman inserted is no doubt what is to be found at
the beginning of the fourth of these unpublished sermons. It is
worth quoting in full:

> That our Blessed Lord and Saviour took upon Him a human
> soul as well as a body is proved, if it be necessary to prove it, by
> His fearing, sorrowing, being in an agony, praying the cup might
> pass from Him, and feeling Himself forsaken by His Father. The
> Son of God in His original nature never could have these feel-
> ings – they are human – they are feelings of a human soul – they
> are not bodily feelings. They are neither of the body, not again
> of the Son of God – they evidence the presence of a human soul,
> which He took to Himself as His own as well as the body, ever
> a perfect manhood – and acted according to it, being inseparably
> united to it, when and as far as He pleased.[14]

The teaching expressed in this sermon is recalled and imagined
in one of Newman's *Discourses to Mixed Congregations*, in 1850.
He called the discourse 'The Mental Sufferings of our Lord in
His Passion', and he pictured Christ's sufferings in vivid

12 ibid., no 407, p. 215.
13 ibid., no 407, p. 216. McGrath has read this faint, pencilled note as
'sorrowing, knowing', but I read it as 'sorrowing, fearing'.
14 Ms. Sermon, 408, McGrath (ed.), *John Henry Newman: Sermons 1824–
1843*, iv, p. 222.

language:

> There He knelt, motionless and still, while the vile and horrible fiend clad His spirit in a robe steeped in all that is hateful and heinous in human crime, which clung close to round His heart, and filled His conscience, and found its way into every sense and pore of His mind, and spread over Him a moral leprosy, till He almost felt Himself to be that which He never could be, and which His foe would fain have made Him (*Mix.* pp. 336–7).

Bearing in mind Newman's awareness of evil as something interior and the significance he placed on heart and mind and conscience, this image of Jesus as a moral leper could hardly be more emphatic. He may not have felt able to speak of him as a human person in the modern sense, but that is what he was in fact describing. Indeed, this passage has led one writer to declare, 'Thus Newman's Christology, for all its adamantine Athanasian orthodoxy, had more of the Epistle to the Hebrews and of nineteenth century humanitarianism in it than, for example, the Tome of Leo', which influenced so decisively the Council of Chalcedon.[15]

There is much more in these sermons, but it is sufficient for our purposes here simply to highlight the key points. We have followed Newman's presentation of Christ as one, as divine, and as human, with his full manhood emphasised by the clear affirmation of the presence in him of a human soul. It is not a matter of assessing the strengths and weaknesses of Newman's Christology – that would be a different exercise – but it is a matter rather of trying to uncover his own understanding of Christ, something that was personal to him, the Christ who penetrated his heart with love.

15 Horton Davies, *Worship and Theology in England iv: from Newman to Martineau (1850–1900)* (Oxford: Oxford University Press, 1962), p. 295.

★

In the Gospels, Jesus tells his disciples that he must leave them. Unless he does so, he says, the Spirit will not come to them (John 16:7). Then, after he has ascended into heaven and the apostles have returned to Jerusalem, we are told that the Spirit descended as wind and fire at Pentecost (Acts 2:2–3). Pentecost is often referred to as the birthday of the Church, and the Church has been spoken of as the temple of the Holy Spirit. Indeed, St Paul asked the Corinthians individually, 'Do you not know that your body is a temple of the Holy Spirit within you?' (1 Corinthians 6:19).

It seems like a process: first the Christ came; after he had died and been raised, he ascended into heaven, and then he sent the Holy Spirit in his place. That, at any rate, is the way people often tend to think. In one of his Anglican sermons, however, Newman took a different view:

> Let us not for a moment suppose that God the Holy Ghost comes in such sense that God the Son remains away. No; He has not so come that Christ does not come, but rather He comes that Christ may come in his coming (*P.S.* vi, p. 126).

In other words, the Spirit has not come as a substitute for the Christ, to compensate for his absence, but rather to make him present, for the Spirit who comes is the Spirit of Christ.

Newman possessed a keen sense of Christ's personal presence in those who believe. Towards the end of his *Lectures on Justification*, which were published in 1838, he described faith as 'colourless, like air or water', as 'the medium through which the soul sees Christ' (*Jfc.* p. 336). Through faith we contemplate Christ, and by faith, he also taught, Christ comes to dwell in us.

A little earlier in those lectures he had spoken of justification, the gift of righteousness, in these terms: 'The Almighty

Father, looking on us, sees not us, but this Sacred Presence, even His dearly beloved Son spiritually manifested in us' (*Jfc*. p. 161). And two years later, when preaching on justification, he echoed the same teaching. At the last day, he remarked, Christ 'will acknowledge Himself, – His image in us, – as though we reflected Him, and He, on looking round about, discerned at once those who were His; those, namely, who gave back to Him His image' (*P.S.* v, 140).

Nor is this teaching simply a notion from the distant past. I am always reminded of it when celebrating Mass on a Sunday in the non-festive seasons, known as Ordinary Time, and using the seventh of the Prefaces that can be used before the Eucharistic Prayer. Addressing the Father, that preface speaks of him sending his Son as our redeemer 'to live like us in all things but sin, *so that you might love in us what you loved in your Son*'.[16] The Father sees the Son made manifest in us.

This understanding of holiness, of the gift of new life, as the personal presence of Christ in the believer was clearly important to Newman. It is a way of speaking about divinisation, about the way human beings can be brought to share in the divine nature. We may recall that the Second Letter of Peter refers to people becoming 'partakers of the divine nature' (2 Peter 1:4). This teaching, of course, played a major part in the fourth-century Arian controversy that so absorbed Newman, but it was significant for himself as well. Preaching in 1839, for example, he had declared that it was 'through the fulness of His Divine Nature' that Christ was able to raise up human infirmity and limitation. He had made human nature his own, 'that so, by God's becoming man, men, through brotherhood with Him, might in the end become as gods' (*P.S.* v, p. 118). It is heady stuff, echoing the classic patristic formula: God became man so that men might become gods. But what does it actually mean?

16 *The Roman Missal* (London: Catholic Truth Society, 2010), p. 618 (my italics).

The formula seems to suggest a kind of parallel: God became human so that human beings might become gods. But we don't, do we? By becoming flesh, the Word did not enable human beings to become further persons in the Godhead. If we are to make any sense of it at all, is this talk of divinisation anything more than poetic licence, an affecting figure of speech?

When we look more closely, we discover that while the formula makes for a punchy soundbite, as we might say, no such simple parallel is in fact being claimed. Instead we find a powerful statement of the significance of Christ's humanity. In his *Essay on Development*, Newman observed that 'in truth, not Christ, but that human nature which He had assumed, was raised and glorified in Him'. And he went on to explain that Christ is in holy people 'because He is in human nature; and he communicates to them that nature, deified by becoming His, that them it may deify' (*Dev.* p. 140). The bestowal of new life occurs precisely through relationship with the humanity that Christ assumed.

If this seems obscure, think of any great human achievement – for example, the setting of a new record. I can remember when Roger Bannister first ran a mile in less than four minutes, though I don't remember the headlines in the newspapers the following day. One probably read, 'Bannister runs four-minute mile'. But another might have read, more starkly, 'Man runs four-minute mile'. Both would have been true. We were celebrating Bannister's particular achievement, but we were also celebrating a human achievement, something that affected us all. He was the only person to have run that distance in so short a period of time – nobody else had – and his record had revealed that human beings could do this. His unique achievement was something that nevertheless everyone shared.

Analogies are never perfect, yet still we may say that when the Word of God was made flesh, when the divine Son became truly human, sharing in what we are, he revealed our human capacity for intimate relationship with what he is. He reveals, in other words, our capacity, such as it may be, for sharing in his divine nature. It was a teaching that recurred regularly in Newman's writing.

Preaching on Easter Sunday in 1831, Newman spoke of Christ as the one who has diffused eternal life. He went on, 'Christ communicates life to us, one by one, by means of that holy and incorrupt nature which He has assumed for our redemption; how, we know not, still, though by an unseen, surely by a real communication of Himself' (*P.S.* ii, p. 145). His human nature was the means of his sharing his life with us.

Some years later Newman emphasised the way Christ's humanity has eternal significance: 'As He became the Atoning Sacrifice by means of His human nature, so He is our High Priest in heaven by means of the same.' This humanity has an essential part to play in gaining salvation for the human race.

> He [Christ] gives us abundantly of His Spirit; but still He gives It not at once from His Divine nature, though from eternity the Holy Ghost proceeds from the Son as well as from the Father, but by means of that incorruptible flesh which He has taken on Him . . . and therefore the streams of life flow to us from Him, as God indeed, but still as God incarnate (*P.S.* vi, pp. 63–4).

Although his divinity is recognised as the ultimate source of human salvation, the immediate source is located in the humanity of Christ, the incorruptible flesh.

Again, in that Good Friday sermon already mentioned, 'The Incarnate Son, a Sufferer and Sacrifice', Newman carried on this line of thought, giving some indication of how this humanity could be a source, and not just the means, of our redemption. Human nature, because it was fallen, needed to atone for its sin, Newman explained. Then he continued:

The Son of God then took our nature on Him, that in Him it might do and suffer what in itself was impossible to it. What it could not effect of itself, it could effect in Him. He carried it about Him through a life of penance. He carried it forward to agony and death. In Him our sinful nature died and rose again. When it died in Him on the cross, that death was its new creation. In Him it satisfied its old and heavy debt; for the presence of His Divinity gave it transcendent merit.

Once more, while the ultimate source of power is the divine nature, the humanity is recognised as immediately instrumental in effecting the salvific work. Christ's human nature is itself a source of power through its union with the Word:

His personal indwelling hallowed it and gave it power. And thus, when it had been offered up upon the Cross, and was made perfect by suffering, it became the first-fruits of a new man; it became a Divine leaven of holiness for the new birth and spiritual life of as many as should receive it (*P.S.* vi.79).

Probably, however, the place where this teaching is best known in Newman's writings occurs in *The Dream of Gerontius*, in the section familiar to many as the hymn, 'Praise to the Holiest in the height'. There Newman spoke of the flesh and blood, the human nature that had failed in Adam, taking up the struggle once again in Christ and prevailing. He referred to a higher gift than grace refining flesh and blood, an idea that has caused some people to ask what gift could be higher than uncreated grace poured into the believer; but Newman was not referring to the believer, but to the Christ. This higher gift than grace was 'God's presence and His very Self, / And Essence all-divine'. And that presence smote the foe 'in man for man' (*V.V.* pp. 363–6). The incarnate Word, sharing our human nature, triumphs in that nature on our behalf.

When Newman spoke of the Christ as our brother and we

through our relationship with him becoming as gods, he was not, therefore, imagining a naïve parallelism between the divine and the human, but affirming rather that the human race is being invited to a share in the divine nature of the Christ because of his share in our humanity. And, if we embrace that relationship, what an effect it has. 'As far as a being can be changed without losing his identity,' he once observed, 'as far as it is sense to say that an existing being can be new created, so far has man this gift when the grace of the Gospel has its perfect work and its maturity of fruit in him' (P.S. v, p. 179). And elsewhere he declared that the saints partake 'each in his own degree of [Christ's] Divine Nature so fully . . . that they are all but Divine, all that they can be made without violating the incommunicable majesty of the Most High' (P.S. viii, p. 253).

Nor does the matter end there. In his *Lectures on Justification*, Newman referred to what happened in Christ when he brought about our salvation as the origin, the beginning, of what now is to be continued in us. The justification Christ won for us consists, Newman said, 'in our new birth'. He went on:

> The Divine Life which raised Him, flowed over and availed unto our rising again from sin and condemnation. It wrought a change in His Sacred Manhood, which became spiritual, without His ceasing to be a man, and was in a wonderful way imparted to us as a new-creating, transforming Power in our hearts (*Jfc.* p. 207).

In other words, the redemption won for the human race by Christ is not something static, merely a gift bestowed, but a reality that should continue within us through his humanity's relationship with ours as something alive and active, transforming the way men and women live.

★

Newman, praying with a pen in his hand, instructed others, as we have seen, to have their hearts penetrated with the love of Christ. Reflecting on his preaching about the Christ, a traditional, orthodox teaching about contemplating Christ as one, as divine, and as human, and appreciating his sense of Christ's personal presence in the believer, who because of his humanity is at one with the human race, saving everyone and exalting them by drawing them to share in his divine nature, we may nevertheless be left feeling that, however inspiring this teaching is intellectually, it leaves us a bit cold. How was Newman praying with a pen in his hand? How might we get a flavour of that?

In 1854, or at about that time, Newman translated the prayer *Anima Christi*. On 29 January 1890, scarcely six months before he died, he sent a copy as a belated Christmas greeting to his occasional correspondent, the evangelical George Edwards. He described it as his Creed. Newman had written:

> Soul of Christ, be my sanctification;
> Body of Christ, be my salvation;
> Blood of Christ, fill all my veins;
> Water of Christ's side, wash out my stains;
> Passion of Christ, my comfort be;
> O good Jesu, listen to me;
> In thy wounds I fain would hide,
> Ne'er to be parted from Thy side;
> Guard me, should the foe assail me;
> Call me when my life shall fail me;
> Bid me come to Thee above,
> With Thy saints to sing Thy love,
> World without end. Amen (*M.D.* p. 352).

The hand holding the pen in prayer expressed what moved the heart.

5

Christ in the Eucharist

Devotion to Christ prompts devotion to the Eucharist. The gift of the Lord's presence in the Eucharist is breathtaking. It must never be underestimated. The value of the reserved sacrament was recognised by the Council of Nicaea in AD 325. It was important that the Eucharist could be taken to those in danger of death. Reservation was a practice that must have been established already, or was coming to be so. And since that time, devotion to the Blessed Sacrament has developed. Catholics will think most obviously of Benediction, of Holy Hours and indeed of Quarant'ore, watching in prayer before the Blessed Sacrament for forty hours; and we also give thanks for the reserved sacrament as a stimulus to private prayer. How did Newman view these matters?

Perhaps there were early stirrings. On 30 November 1817, he wrote a prayer of thanksgiving for his faith. It was the day he received his first Communion in the chapel of Trinity College, Oxford. Sixty years later, in 1877, he wrote a memorandum in which he referred to a photograph he looked at each day. It was of that college chapel. He observed, 'I look at that communion table, and recollect with what feelings I went up to it in November 1817 for my first communion.'[1] As an Anglican, of course, without formally accepting Catholic teaching on transubstantiation, he acquired a keen sense of the reality of Christ's presence in the Eucharist.

1 Quoted in Pascal Murray OSB, *Newman the Oratorian* (Dublin: Gill and Macmillan, 1969), p. 60.

In 1838 he preached a sermon which he called 'The Eucharistic Presence' (*P.S.* vi, pp. 138–52). It contained two passages – one at the beginning, the other towards the end – that are particularly striking. At the beginning he expressed his understanding of eucharistic presence as a spiritual presence, and then explained immediately what he meant:

> We call His presence in this Holy Sacrament a spiritual presence, not as if 'spiritual' were but a name or mode of speech, and He were really absent, but by way of expressing that He who is present there can neither be seen nor heard; that He cannot be approached or ascertained by any of the senses; that He is not present in place, that He is not present carnally, though He is really present.

The presence is real, though not detected by our senses. And Newman added, quite characteristically, 'And how this is, of course is a mystery' (*P.S.* vi, pp. 136–7). Then, as the sermon drew to a close, he encouraged his congregation to pray for a deeper insight into the mystery of the incarnation so as to desire and find in the Eucharist a reflection, a type of that mystery. He continued:

> No one realizes the Mystery of the Incarnation but must feel disposed towards that of Holy Communion. Let us pray Him to give us an earnest longing after Him – a thirst for his presence – and anxiety to find Him – a joy on hearing that He is to be found, even now, under the veil of sensible things, – and a good hope that *we* shall find Him there. Blessed indeed are they who have not seen, and yet have believed (*P.S.* vi, p. 151).

So Newman as an Anglican had this acute awareness of the reality of Christ's presence in the Eucharist. All the same, it seems, he was unaware of the reserved sacrament.

After being received as a Catholic in October 1845, he stayed on in the village of Littlemore on the outskirts of Oxford until the following February. At that time, Littlemore was part of the parish of the university church, St Mary the Virgin, and so Newman, as vicar, was responsible for its care. He had moved there himself in 1842 to reflect and take stock of his position in the Church of England and loved living there. He had built its church to serve the pastoral needs of the area. His mother had laid the foundation stone in 1835 and the church was consecrated on 22 September the following year.

When he left Littlemore, he was emotional. As he told his former curate and lifelong friend, William Copeland, he had had to tear himself away, kissing some of the furniture, the bed and the mantlepiece (*L.D.* xi, p. 132 [215]). He moved to Maryvale, close to Oscott College.

A week later, on 1 March 1846, he wrote to his friend, Elizabeth Bowden, the widow of John Bowden who had been his earliest and closest friend as an undergraduate at Trinity. Whatever his sadness at leaving Littlemore, there was, he had discovered, one compensation. He spoke to her delightedly about the reserved sacrament and, as he said, 'the surpassing privilege of having a Chapel under the very roof in which I live [at Maryvale] and Christ in it'. And it seems that this privilege, as he called it, was to him a novelty, because he went on to explain that, before his conversion, when he had been abroad in Rome in 1833, he had 'abstained from acts of worship', neither understanding nor trying to understand the Mass; and he added, 'I did not know, or did not observe, the tabernacle Lamp' (*L.D.* xi, p. 131).

In those earlier days, therefore, the significance of the reserved sacrament seems to have passed him by. However, it was evidently something that had come to mean much to him. Indeed, some days earlier, on 26 February, he had written to another close friend, Henry Wilberforce, who was still an Anglican priest at that time, although he and his wife and family would become Catholics in 1850. Newman told him:

I am writing next room to the Chapel – It is such an incomprehensible blessing to have Christ in bodily presence in one's house, within one's walls, as swallows up all other privileges and destroys, or should destroy, every pain. To know that He is close by – to be able again and again through the day to go in to Him; and be sure my dearest W[ilberforce], when I am thus in His Presence you are not forgotten. It is *the* place for intercession surely, where the Blessed Sacrament is (*L.D.* xi, p,129 [214]).

We hear in those words his sense of wonder at being in the Lord's presence and the consolation that he found there. As Newman was described as being never less alone than when alone – *numquam minus solus quam cum solus* – it is not difficult to imagine how he would have relished the power of silence and stillness when he made a visit to the Blessed Sacrament.

Nor should we suppose, by the way, that his words to Wilberforce were simply the enthusiastic outburst of a new convert. Seven years later, after he had been found guilty, however unjustly, of libelling Giacinto Achilli, the immoral former Dominican friar who had been brought to England to attack Catholics, and while he was waiting to be sentenced, he was persuaded to stay and rest with his friends, the Hope-Scotts, at Abbotsford in Scotland. To his happy surprise, he found that there was a chapel in their home as well. Lord and Lady Arundel were staying at the same time. In a letter he wrote on 7 January 1853 to Father John Joseph Gordon at the Birmingham Oratory, he commented that he did not know which of the two couples, the Hope-Scotts or the Arundels, was in the chapel most:

I suppose they are ordinarily there at four stated times of the day (including Mass) and for a good long space each time. Indeed it is impossible to be in a more simply religious house, which was not a convent. Some of the servants, I see, come in to visit the Blessed Sacrament and the communions have been very good during the Christmas season.

And he concluded:

> I have not noticed this great compensation of my banishment, which I could hardly have expected any where, an altar, nay the Blessed Sacrament in the House. I had no hope of the Blessed Sacrament and was quite taken by surprise, when I heard it – and everything is as it should be for the service of the Altar (*L.D.* xv, p. 248 [275]).

A sense of his own devotion to the Blessed Sacrament, something habitual, is unmistakable.

The following year, on St David's Day, 1 March, he composed prayers for a short visit to the Blessed Sacrament. They were found among his papers after his death and published in *Meditations and Devotions*. They capture prayerfully so much of what his sermons had already explained. He began by placing himself in the Lord's presence, but at the same time, with a characteristic twist, acknowledging that he was already there: 'I place myself in the presence of Him, in whose Incarnate Presence I am before I place myself there.' Next, he addressed the incarnate Lord, 'I adore Thee, O my Saviour, present here as God and man, in soul and body, in true flesh and blood.' And then he continued:

> I acknowledge and confess that I kneel before that Sacred Humanity, which was conceived in Mary's womb, and lay in Mary's bosom; which grew up to man's estate, and by the Sea of Galilee called the Twelve, wrought miracles, and spoke words of wisdom and peace; which in due season hung on the cross, lay in the tomb, rose from the dead, and now reigns in heaven.

These words of prayer seem to echo his preaching. And he concluded with a profession of faith: 'I praise, and bless, and give myself wholly to Him, who is the true bread of my soul, and my everlasting joy' (*M.D.* pp. 391–2).

★

Wonderful as the eucharistic presence is and invaluable as a way of stimulating prayer among people and an awareness of Christ's presence, all is not simple and straightforward. In an instruction issued in 1967 to assist the implementation of the teaching of the Second Vatican Council and with reference to exposition of the Blessed Sacrament, there was a warning: 'Care must be taken that during these expositions the worship given to the Blessed Sacrament should be seen, by signs, in its relation to the Mass.'[2] In other words, if our devotion to the Eucharist becomes too fixed, too static, we may come to give to the consecrated host an undue priority and so we may lose sight of it as a fruit of the Mass and so lose sight as well of the vibrant dynamic relationship that should be at the core of our devotion.

Sacrosanctum Concilium, the Dogmatic Constitution on the Sacred Liturgy, had spoken of the Eucharist as 'a sacrament of faithful relationships, a sign of unity, a bond of divine love, a special Easter meal': relationships, unity, bond and meal; expressions that ring out and touch the heart. And it had introduced that stirring description by declaring: 'Our Saviour inaugurated the eucharistic sacrifice of his body and blood at the last supper on the night he was betrayed, in order to make his sacrifice of the cross last throughout time until he should return'.[3] The gift is given to last throughout time. Christ's presence is an abiding presence.

What connection does this have with John Henry Newman a century earlier?

---

2 *Eucharisticum Mysterium*, III, v.
3 *Sacrosanctum Concilium*, n. 47. Norman P. Tanner, (ed.), *Decrees of the Ecumenical Councils* ii (London: Sheed & Ward, 1990), p. 830.

In 1893, when William Neville produced *Meditations and Devotions* from the cardinal's papers, he included a meditation, probably dated around 1860, called, 'Jesus Our Daily Sacrifice'. Newman had written:

> Our Lord not only offered Himself as a Sacrifice on the Cross, but He makes Himself a perpetual, a daily sacrifice, to the end of time. In the Holy Mass that One Sacrifice on the Cross once offered is renewed, continued, applied to our benefit. He seems to say, My Cross was raised up 1800 years ago, and only for a few hours – and very few of my servants were present there – but I intend to bring millions into my Church. For their sakes then I will perpetuate my Sacrifice, that each of them may be as though they had severally been present on Calvary. I will offer myself up day by day to the Father, that every one of my followers may have the opportunity to offer his petitions to Him, sanctified and recommended by the all-meritorious virtue of my Passion. Thus I will be a Priest for ever, – after the order of Melchisedech – My priests shall stand at the Altar – but not they, but I rather will offer. I will not let them offer mere bread and wine, but I myself will be present upon the Altar instead, and I will offer up myself invisibly, while they perform the outward rite. And thus the Lamb that was slain once for all, though He is ascended on high, ever remains a victim from His miraculous presence in Holy Mass under the figure and appearance of mere earthly and visible symbols (*M.D.*, pp. 291–2).

The passage is long, but it captures clearly the sense of the Mass as an action, an abiding, perpetual sacrifice which, as we have seen, was integral to the teaching of the Second Vatican Council, a sacrifice made possible by Christ's presence – 'I myself will be present upon the Altar' – a presence that is the fundamental to eucharistic adoration and devotion.

There are two other concepts mentioned, which will repay closer attention.

★

Consider first what Newman said about the altar, imagining Jesus speaking: 'My priests shall stand at the Altar . . . but I myself will be present upon the Altar.'

If Catholic devotion to the Lord's real presence in the Eucharist, however praiseworthy, can nevertheless become too fixed and static, running the risk of neglecting the personal bond between Christ and the believer, as that 1967 Instruction implied, a further aspect of that flaw is revealed, to put it simply, when churches come to be regarded first and foremost as homes for housing the Blessed Sacrament. Think, for example, of the outcry from time to time in parishes when a church is reordered and the tabernacle moved from the high altar to a side chapel. But churches are not built principally to house tabernacles; they are built to celebrate liturgy.

What is particularly intriguing is to notice that the church Newman had built at Littlemore in 1836 has been regarded as the first Tractarian church. And it is possible to say what made it distinctive. It has been described as showing 'the Catholic feeling of a church', as it made 'the altar rather than the pulpit . . . the central point of worship'.[4] The altar was central. The church itself has, of course, been developed and extended since, but at that time, as Sheridan Gilley has observed, the building 'with a raised chancel, a stone altar with some handsome carved work and a central recess behind it with a cross, represented rank Popery to some'. Gilley continued, 'The prominence given to the altar was a very cautious step towards that radical liturgical and sacramental reordering which was to transform hitherto pulpit- and preacher-dominated churches

4 See Alf Härdelin, *The Tractarian Understanding of the Eucharist* (Uppsala: University Press, 1965), p. 269.

all over England.'[5] So, in Littlemore, in the first church that Newman had built – there were to be others, in Birmingham and in Dublin – although still an Anglican and, indeed, at the height of his influence in the Oxford Movement, his instinct for Catholic liturgy was revealed.

The prominence he gave to the altar was not by chance. Preaching in St Mary the Virgin in Oxford on 31 May 1835 – it was the Sunday after the feast of the Ascension – and explaining the need for a church to be built at Littlemore, he spoke first about churches in general as places through which 'in a certain sense we realize the unseen world and bring down heaven upon earth'. Here again we hear Newman's sense of the link between what is seen and what is unseen. And then he guided his listeners, going forward through a church from its baptismal font to the pulpit. But he did not stop there, and continued:

> We go forward still, and we come to the holy altar where Christ manifests Himself in His highest and most mysterious blessings. As we realize His presence all over the Church, so here we realize it especially. We consider it to be the holiest part of the Church because He works His holiest wonder there.[6]

The altar is supreme. And while Newman refers to this presence in this sermon as invisible, seen and adored only by faith, when he preached the following year, on 23 October, both in the morning in St Mary the Virgin and later that afternoon in his by then recently opened church in Littlemore, he returned to the theme still more emphatically, declaring the altar to be 'the most sacred part of the Church'. Why? He explained:

5 Gilley, *Newman and His Age*, p. 156.
6 Ms Sermon, no 388, McGrath (ed.) *John Henry Newman: Sermons 1824–1843*, iv, p. 93.

On the Altar is consecrated the Holy Body and Blood of Christ
– He becomes present there in a way in which He is no where
else present except in the faithful hearts who receive Him –
therefore we fittingly look to the Altar, as the source and foun-
tain from which His precious blood is dispensed to us
separately.[7]

The altar is the *locus* for the eucharistic liturgy, the place where
Christ's presence is made real among those who have gathered.
As an Anglican, as we have noticed, Newman would speak of
this presence as spiritual, but not meaning a way of being
present that compensated for absence. He meant rather that
what was spiritual was real, without being accessible to the
senses (see *P.S.* vi, pp. 136–7).

And what Newman was preaching, this stress on eucharistic
liturgy, he also put into practice. On 9 April 1837 he began a
weekly Communion Service. He wrote to his sister, Harriett,
some weeks later, 'I began weekly communion at Easter, and
have found the Church very well attended. I have it at seven in
the morning. Last Sunday I had thirty six communicants' (*L.D.*
vi, p. 65).

★

The second concept to notice from Newman's meditation on
Jesus' daily sacrifice is that of 'symbol': 'The Lamb that was slain
once for all remains a victim from His miraculous presence in
Holy Mass under the figure and appearance of mere earthly and
visible symbols.' 'Symbol' to Catholic ears can often sound rather
hollow or empty, something arbitrary, distinct from the reality it
signifies. What is particularly noteworthy, however, is to recall
the influence on Newman of the Romantic movement. And for
the Romantic poets like Coleridge and Wordsworth, symbols

7 Ms Sermon, no 427, McGrath (ed.) *John Henry Newman: Sermons
1824–1843*, iv, p. 249.

were anything but empty and arbitrary, distinct from what they symbolised. On the contrary, for them, symbols participated in the reality that they symbolised.[8] They have a sacramental quality to them. The eucharistic symbols too, therefore, share in the reality that they symbolise. They participate in it.

In 1831, preaching at Easter on 'Christ, a Quickening Spirit', Newman declared that before Christ 'went away, He remembered our necessity, and completed His work, bequeathing to us a special mode of approaching Him, a Holy Mystery, in which we receive (we know not how) the virtue of that Heavenly Body, which is the life of all that believe.'

Here already Newman was indicating his conviction that what the Lord had done for humanity was to be made available 'to the end of time'. And how was this to be accomplished? This Anglican sermon continued that it is through 'the blessed Sacrament of the Eucharist, in which "Christ is evidently set forth crucified among us;" that we, feasting upon the Sacrifice, may be "partakers of the Divine Nature."' Shortly afterwards he added, 'Christ communicates life to us, one by one, by means of that holy and incorrupt nature which He assumed for our redemption; how, we know not; still, though by an unseen, surely by a real communication of Himself.' And he went on to quote an array of passages from the discourse on the Bread of Life in the Fourth Gospel, most notably, 'I am the living Bread which came down from heaven; if any man eat of this bread, he shall live for ever: and the Bread that I will give is My flesh, which I will give for the life of the world.' And again: 'Whoso eateth My flesh, and drinketh My blood, hath eternal life; and I will raise him up at the last day' (*P.S.* ii, pp. 144–6).

Newman was an indefatigable editor of his own writings. He was forever correcting and improving what he had

8 See Stephen Prickett, *Romanticism and Religion* (Cambridge: Cambridge University Press, 1976).

written. In this last instance, was he really leaning so heavily towards Catholic teaching as early as 1831? It is hard to say, although in his *Apologia* he remarked that his great friend, Hurrell Froude, influenced him 'gradually to believe in the Real Presence' (*Apo.* p. 25 [35]). How far that influence had reached by 1831 is unclear, but this was certainly the text that he published as an Anglican before he was received as a Catholic. And its essential message is developed in one of the sermons he preached while Rector of the Catholic university in Dublin in the 1850s.

On the Sunday after the feast of the Epiphany in 1857, he preached on 'Omnipotence in Bonds'. It is naturally enough a sermon on the incarnation. He reflected with his congregation on the Word becoming flesh, God becoming man, 'the Highest', as he said, 'became the lowest, the Creator took His place among His own creatures, Power became weakness, and Wisdom looked to men like folly' (*O.S.* p. 76). The Lord of all became subject to all, even to accepting humiliation, torture and execution. The omnipotent Lord of all was in bonds.

Then Newman made another of those imaginative leaps, so characteristic of his thinking and writing. He spoke of Christ 'perpetuating His captivity to the end of the world'. He was speaking, of course, of the Eucharist, and he referred once more to symbols: 'The great truth is daily before our eyes,' he said. 'He has ordained the standing miracle of His Body and Blood under visible symbols, that He may secure thereby the standing mystery of Omnipotence in bonds.' He referred to the institution of the Eucharist and then continued:

Henceforth, He is in the hands of sinners once more. Frail, ignorant, sinful man, by the sacerdotal power given to him, compels the presence of the Highest; he lays Him up in a small tabernacle; he dispenses Him to a sinful people. Those who are only just now cleansed from mortal sin, open their lips for

Him; those who are soon to return to mortal sin, receive Him
into their breasts; those who are polluted with vanity and self-
ishness and ambition and pride, presume to make him their
guest; the frivolous, the tepid, the worldly minded, fear not to
welcome Him. Alas! alas! even those who wish to be more in
earnest, entertain Him with cold and wandering thoughts, and
quench that Love which would inflame them with Its own fire,
did they but open to It (*O.S.* p. 87).

The style and tone of this passage may not be common among
us today and should not stir us to morbid scrupulosity, but it
has its own power and beauty. In the Eucharist the Lord has
continued to place himself at our mercy. His sacrifice is perpetual. It lasts throughout time.

★

Approaches to the Eucharist are notoriously controversial, and
there were eucharistic and liturgical controversies that besieged
Newman in his Anglican days. But when we explore his
thought from the more personal angle, we discover the depth
of his own devotion to Christ's presence in the Eucharist. Yet
that devotion was not static or fixed; it was alive, flowing from
his sense of the redemption won for humanity on Calvary and
made really present throughout time whenever Mass is celebrated. In the words of Pope Leo the Great, 'The visible presence of our Redeemer passed over into sacraments.'[9] All the
sacraments, but the sacrament of the Eucharist in an outstanding way, connect earth with heaven.

In his book, *Christ the Sacrament of the Encounter with God*,
which was published first in 1960 but must have been largely
written before Pope John announced that there was to be another
Vatican Council, the Dominican theologian, Edward

9 See Pope Leo the Great, Sermon 2 on the Ascension, *The Divine
Office* ii (London: Collins, 1974), p. 642.

Schillebeeckx, explained that 'if Christ did not make his heavenly bodiliness visible in some way in our earthly sphere, his redemption would after all no longer be for us; redemption would no longer turn its face towards us. Then the human mediation of Christ would be meaningless.'[10] But the incarnation, and so the humanity of Christ, we must always remember, has eternal significance. Schillebeeckx made it plain that 'Christ makes his presence among us actively visible and tangible too, not directly through his own bodiliness, but by extending among us on earth in visible form the function of his bodily reality which is in heaven.' And he then stated, 'This precisely is what the sacraments are: the earthly extension of the "body of the Lord". This is the Church.'[11] Christ is the sacrament of the Father; the Church is the sacrament of Christ; and the individual sacraments – and supremely the Eucharist through the identification of the consecrated elements with the Lord's body and blood, soul and divinity – establish Christ's presence among us throughout time, connecting time with eternity, earth with heaven.

Reflecting on these thoughts is not meant to imply that what Newman wrote anticipates explicitly what Schillebeeckx has explained so clearly, but his line of thought is moving instinctively in the same direction, affirming a perpetual, daily sacrifice that lasts to the end of time. As we have already noticed, he had declared in his Anglican days, 'Before [the Lord] went away, He remembered our necessity, and *completed* His work, bequeathing to us a special mode of approaching Him . . . This is the blessed Sacrament of the Eucharist' (*P.S.* ii, p. 144).

10 Edward Schillebeeckx, *Christ the Sacrament of the Encounter with God* (London: Sheed & Ward, 1963), p. 43.
11 ibid., p. 41.

6

At prayer

When Newman became a cardinal in 1879, he was able to have a private chapel at the Birmingham Oratory. It is a section of his study and remains to this day as it was, a kind of shrine. What may strike the visitor as most noticeable is the number of pictures on the walls around the altar. They are mainly of his family and friends, people whom he held in prayer. The prayer of intercession was important for him.

When Dom Placid Murray published Newman's Oratorian papers, entitled *Newman the Oratorian*, in 1969, which contained principally the addresses he had given to the community at Birmingham, he began the book with a long study of Newman as a priest. The fourth chapter, 'Prayer and Ministry', brings out very clearly the place of intercessory prayer in Newman's life. He explains that there are notebooks of Newman's, preserved in the Oratory, in which he stated his intentions, praying, for example, for 'singleness of heart', for 'simple dependence on the grace of Christ' and for 'liveliness and fervency of prayer'.

He listed as well the people he wished to pray for, including those 'Dear to me; Kind to me; Cold to me; No how to me', for family and parishioners, including parishioners from St Mary the Virgin and Littlemore, for Protestants as well as Catholics, for Irish friends, for converts and for those who had died. He seemed to forget no one, including, for instance, Manning's young wife, Caroline, who had died in 1837. He prayed as well for his brother Charles, his sister Harriett, his friends John Keble and Bishop David Moriarty of Kerry, and also those with whom he had sometimes clashed, like Samuel Wilberforce and Richard Whately. It is an intriguing list.

Remembering in prayer those who had died on the anniversary of their death was plainly for Newman a lifelong habit. As Murray concluded, '[Newman] carried over in prayer into his Catholic life in 1846, at the very moment of setting out for the continent en route to Rome, all his Anglican friends and associates who had been the objects of his prayer in 1840 and 1845.'[1] Interceding for others mattered to him.

The principal text on intercessory prayer in Newman's writings is a sermon he preached in 1835. He called it, simply, 'Intercession' (P.S. iii, pp. 350–66). He began by encouraging his congregation to pray for themselves – 'Ask and it shall be given to us' – and for others, and he declared, 'Intercession is the characteristic of Christian worship, the privilege of the heavenly adoption, the exercise of the perfect and spiritual mind' (P.S. iii, pp. 350–1). No wonder he prized it so highly. And he went on to explain that intercession is a special duty for Christians, who must pray for themselves and for each other because Christianity is 'a social religion' (P.S. iii, pp. 352–3), and that it is the prayers of the holy that are efficacious: 'Intercession is never more appropriate than when sin had been utterly abolished, and the heart was most affectionate and least selfish' (P.S. iii, p. 354). He illuminated his case with a whole range of scriptural passages. Moreover, he argued, intercession is efficacious because those who intercede are people of faith. Christ has saved us by interceding for us and he bestows upon those who believe 'that privilege which implies and involves all others, and brings [them] into nearest resemblance to Himself, the privilege of Intercession' (P.S. iii, p. 362). It is evident that Newman valued this way of praying. As Placid Murray

---

1 Murray, *Newman the Oratorian*, pp. 61–3. See also Trevor, *Newman: Light in Winter*, p. 630.

remarked, his 'habit of prayer, practised from boyhood, remained constantly with him, and . . . seems to have continued along the same lines, without any break, from his Anglican to his Catholic life'. He added, 'This prayer was predominantly intercessory.'[2]

I have no wish to dispute that conclusion. Any account of Newman at prayer must take the importance he attached to intercession with the utmost seriousness. Nevertheless, I believe there is more to be said. There are strands to be woven together.

★

Consider, first, Newman's personality. He confessed to his friend John Capes in 1868, 'I have often been puzzled at myself, that I should be both particularly fond of being alone, and particularly fond of being with friends, yet I know both the one and the other are true' (*L.D.* xxiv, p. 53 [429]). He delighted in the company of his friends, but he was content in his own company as well. He was described, as we have noticed, as being never less alone than when alone – *numquam minus solus quam cum solus*. Newman was at ease with solitude.

Fundamental for him was that first conversion in 1816, bringing him 'to the thought of two and two only absolute and luminously self-evident beings, myself and my Creator' (*Apo.* p. 4, [17–18]). Those words from his *Apologia*, describing that youthful experience, were anticipated sixteen years earlier when, in a meditation he composed in 1848, he prayed to God as the blessedness of the soul. 'To enjoy the sight of Thee is the only happiness of eternity,' he wrote. 'God and my soul will be the only two beings left in the whole world, as far as I am concerned. He will be all in all, whether I wish it or no' (*M.D.* pp. 442–3). He possessed this overwhelming sense of the reality of God.

2 Murray, *Newman the Oratorian*, p. 69.

Then, as we know from William Neville, Newman prayed with a pen in his hand. His *Meditations and Devotions*, like the one we noticed earlier, bear witness to that. But as we read what he has written, it is hard not to wonder at the depths from which those prayers have arisen. He did not just sit down and scribble immediately. In a letter in 1869 to John Hayes, an Anglican priest in Shropshire, he explained that he often wrote chapters over and over again. 'I am not stating this as a merit,' he observed, 'only that some persons write their best first, and I very seldom do.' And he continued shortly afterwards that 'my one and single desire and aim has been to do what is so difficult – viz. to express clearly and exactly my meaning' (*L.D.* xxiv, p. 241 [434]).

What was true for his books and sermons must have been true for these meditations and devotions as well. The pen in the hand did not mean that the right words came without effort. So, while words were being committed to paper, there must also have been long, careful thought. Riding out on that May morning in 1828 after his sister Mary's death, and appreciating the opportunity to be away from Oxford, he was nevertheless, we remember, touched with sadness and a sense of life's transitory nature. He was pondering, reflecting.[3] Newman, who loved his friends, valued solitude and was gripped by a sense of the divine presence.

A Christmas sermon that he called 'Equanimity' and preached in 1839 offers an image that seems to suggest experience. He asked, 'Did you ever look at an expanse of water, and observe the ripples on the surface? Do you think that disturbance penetrates below it?' He answered, no, and then continued:

> You have seen or heard of fearful tempests on the sea; scenes of horror and distress, . . . Yet even these violent commotions do

3 See typescript in chapter 2, pp. 24–5.

74

not reach into the depths. The foundations of the ocean, the vast depths of water which girdle the earth, are as tranquil and as silent in the storm as in a calm.

Then he observed, 'So it is with the souls of holy men. They have a well of peace springing up within them unfathomable; and though the accidents of the hour may make them seem agitated, yet in their hearts they are not so.'

Shortly afterwards he added that:

the Christian has a deep, silent, hidden peace, which the world sees not, – like some well in a retired and shady place, difficult of access. He is the greater part of his time by himself, and when he is in solitude, that is his real state. What he is when left to himself and to his God, that is his true life (*P.S.* v, p. 69).

Newman would not have been identifying himself as a holy man – we have seen him say, 'I have nothing of a Saint about me' – yet it may be that this image, even subconsciously, described his disposition, or at least what he aspired to: solitude and stillness, and a depth of peace in the presence of God.

In 1978 Sister Wendy Beckett, the hermit and art historian, wrote a short article which she called, 'Simple Prayer'. Prayer, she pointed out, is not simple because it is easy, but because it is uncomplicated. 'The essential act of prayer', she explained, 'is to stand unprotected before God.' Then she asked, 'What will God do?' And she answered immediately, 'He will take possession of us.' I think Newman would have loved that, particularly because she then goes on to say, 'That he should [take possession of us] is the whole purpose of life.'[4] Or, as Newman had observed, what Christians are when left to themselves and to their God, that is their true life.

4 Wendy Beckett, 'Simple Prayer', *The Clergy Review* lxiii (February 1978), pp. 42–5; quotation on p. 43.

And in that stillness and solitude, alert to the divine presence and before picking up his pen, what was Newman doing? He was contemplating. We need to weave in other strands.

*

First, there is longing. When we pray, what do we truly desire? What we want is crucial. In her article, Wendy Beckett stated, 'Prayer is prayer if we want it to be.' She continued, 'Ask yourself: What do I really want when I pray? Do you want to be possessed by God?' And then she added, with dry good humour, 'Or, to put the question more honestly, do you want to want it?' How many people would reply that actually, they don't, but they wish they did. And she concluded, 'Then you have it.'[5]

What we truly desire is the key. Prayer is prayer if we want it to be. We remember Newman's words to his parishioners in 1838, speaking about the link between the incarnation and the Eucharist and encouraging them to pray for 'an earnest longing after Him – a thirst for His presence – and anxiety to find Him' (*P.S.* vi, p. 151).[6] Longing, thirst, anxiety: when we pray, what do we truly desire? We may feel feeble and inadequate. But deep down, in spite of our diffidence, is there that desire for intimacy with the Lord, that longing and thirst, and even anxiety?

Then, as well as longing, there is mystery. Newman was sensitive to mystery. In those 1836 sermons on the incarnation, before launching into his exposition of the doctrine, he began by inviting those listening to him to contemplate. Initially he was critical. 'When persons find they cannot understand the mysteries of the gospel,' he noted, 'when they cannot understand *how* the things are, earthly and heavenly, which are set before us therein, they not infrequently turn away from them

5 Beckett, 'Simple Prayer', p. 43.
6 See chapter 5, p. 58.

altogether and will not look at them or contemplate them.' However, he affirmed, 'The trial of faith is steadily to look though we do not understand.' Those who are impatient, refusing to contemplate, dismiss gazing on the mysteries as systematising, curiosity or speculation. He went on:

> On the other hand, the humble Christian will find great comfort and a devout pleasure in *contemplating* the gospel mysteries – especially that about which most is told us, the Incarnation – not that we can understand any part of it, but still we can eye the doctrine, embrace it, dwell and feed upon it.

The idea could scarcely be more graphic: to eye the doctrine, embrace it, dwell and feed upon it. Newman may have prayed with a pen in his hand, but the pen was not there to solve the mystery. It was not an instrument to explain a mystery's mechanics. Newman was emphatic:

> Let this difference be clearly kept in view – the difference between understanding how a thing is, and seeing that it is. To attempt to explain how God became man, would be very profane – but to state clearly the fact, to view it in its parts, to place it before the eye of the mind as a picture, this God allows, injoins us – for this God has supplied materials in Scripture, this God has enabled us to do by the clear and complete teaching of His Holy Church Catholic from the first.[7]

And then, in this sermon and those that follow, as we have seen, he launched into his account of the incarnation, considering the Christ as one, as divine, and as human.

This way of encouraging contemplation was a common feature of Newman's approach to the mysteries of faith, not presuming to solve them, but inviting people instead to gaze

7 Ms. Sermon, no 405, pp. 1–2.

on the parts, one by one. This method recurs in his work time and again. In his study of Trinitarian doctrine, particularly in relation to the Arian controversy, he explained that:

> one image corrects another; and the accumulation of images is not, as is so often thought, the restless and fruitless effort of the mind to *enter into the Mystery*, but is a *safeguard* against any one image, nay any collection of images, being supposed *adequate* (*Ath.* ii. p. 445).

In his critique of rationalism in its attempts to tame mystery, he spoke of revelation as 'religious doctrine viewed on its illuminated side; a Mystery is the selfsame doctrine viewed on the side unilluminated'. 'Revelation, in this way of considering it,' he said, 'is not a revealed system, but consists of a number of detached and incomplete truths belonging to a vast system unrevealed, of doctrines and injunctions mysteriously connected together' (*Ess.* i, pp. 41–2). Then, in *A Grammar of Assent*, he referred to the way in which, while theology has to review many propositions, 'Religion has to do with the real, and the real is particular.' Theology examines many propositions and their relationship with one another, while religion reflects on each of the propositions that compose it separately, 'and lives and thrives in the contemplation of them' (*G.A.* p. 140 [94–5]).

In the sermon Newman preached on 17 April 1836, immediately before this series on the incarnation, which was really a sermon on theological method and against rationalising, he stated, 'Surely it is *as* true that the Word is God as if Jesus Christ were not the Word; and it is as true that Jesus Christ is the Word, as if the Word were not God.' What is required is 'steadily [to] take hold of and keep fast hold of each truth by itself'.[8]

8 Ms. Sermon, no 404, 14, McGrath (ed.), *John Henry Newman: Sermons 1824–1843*, iv, p. 111.

More than thirty years later, on 3 February 1867, he made the same point in a letter to an unknown correspondent who had complained about the vagueness and obscurity of dogmatic language. Newman replied that he was confusing dogma and theology. Theology, he explained, is scientific and difficult, but dogmatic propositions are not. He gave various examples, among them, 'Jesus Christ is God' and 'Jesus Christ is man'. When these dogmas are compared, then there will indeed be questioning, argument and more, but these statements in themselves, he declared, are simple and each one can be received 'by a child or a village old woman' (*L.D.* xxiii, p. 51).

Contemplating aspects of the mystery one by one can never solve the puzzle intellectually. It is not meant to. Instead, it touches the heart and makes the mystery real. So Newman urged people to contemplate the Christ, to gaze on him – one, divine, and human – so that the impact of the mystery could become real for them.

★

Newman's contemplative approach to mystery is not, of course, unique to him. Art offers an analogy. Let me return briefly to Sister Wendy Beckett. In 1993 she produced a book called *The Gaze of Love*. It contained a series of forty pictures, and she supplied a short commentary on each. One in particular caught my eye. It is called 'Living Memory (Diptych) 1988', by the British-born artist Maria Chevska. It is a canvas in two parts, which, Beckett commented, are 'both equally baffling'. On the left there is perhaps a delicate cloth hanging from a branch or a bare back; on the right, 'a tender medley of colour and shape', from which, as we gaze, images may emerge. We struggle to find a meaning, but the artist's 'reverent attention to memory that is alive and life that is remembered', according to Beckett, draws from the artist and the silent viewer the state of prayer. There are secrets here to which we do not have access, but God has access. God's presence is silent, Beckett continued, validating the silence of the artist and the viewer and sweeping us 'beyond our narrow certainties into the freedom of infinite truth'. She concluded:

> And yet to verbalize all this is at once to diminish its power. If we are to live in God and be remembered by Him, we have to sacrifice the self-importance of control and explicit explanations. All we need to do here is to contemplate.[9]

We gaze at the parts, contemplating humbly. It is a startlingly remarkable echo of Newman's approach.

Prayer can take many forms. Intercession has a vital part to play. As Newman urged, we must pray for one another. And he prayed with a pen in his hand, translating his praying into prayers written down. What was written, however, was the fruit of contemplation, the longing and thirst for the divine presence, eyed, embraced, dwelt and fed upon.

Some sentences towards the end of *Meditations and Devotions* perhaps capture most clearly his disposition. He prayed, 'Make me then like Thyself, O my God, since, in spite of myself, such Thou canst make me, such I can be made.' Then, 'Let me be partaker of that Divine Nature in all the riches of Its attributes, which in fulness of substance and in personal presence became the Son of Mary.' And his conclusion is breathtaking: 'Enter my heart substantially and personally, and fill it with fervour by filling it with Thee . . . Thou art the living Flame, and ever burnest with love of man: enter into me and set me on fire after Thy pattern and likeness' (*M.D.* pp. 596, 597, 599). Newman was no dry academic.

9 Wendy Beckett, *The Gaze of Love: Meditations on Art* (London: Marshall Pickering, 1993), p. 32.

7

In darkness

'It was like coming into port after a rough sea.' That was the image Newman used to describe his 1845 conversion to Catholicism. 'And', he continued, 'my happiness on that score remains to this day without interruption.' He affirmed that since that time he had had 'no anxiety of heart'; he had been 'in perfect peace and contentment' and without a single doubt. He was not conscious that his conversion had brought about any change, 'moral or intellectual', in his mind, or that it had made his faith firmer in the fundamental truths of revelation or himself more fervent (see *Apo.* p. 238 [214]). Stating this unwavering conviction was vital for him.

From Newman's earliest days as a Catholic, doubts and questions had been raised by others. As early as 1848, for example, Henry Bourne, the father of Francis Bourne, the future Cardinal Archbishop of Westminster, had written to him because of rumours he had heard that Newman was dissatisfied as a Catholic (see *L.D.* xii, p. 218 [234–5]). And in 1862 the *Lincolnshire Express* published an advertisement signed by G. Noel Hoare, asking, 'What has become of John Henry Newman?' The advertisement reported, in answer to its own question, that Newman had been living unhappily in Paris, having become utterly sceptical, and was ridiculing the Roman religion.

Newman replied to put the record straight, and asked in his turn, 'Who is this Mr G. Noel Hoare? In an age of light, where has the unfortunate man been living? . . . What bad luck has seduced him into print?' (*L.D.* xx, p. 208 [338–40]).

A few days later on 27 June, when *The Globe*, at the time a Whig newspaper, had also printed a piece about rumours that he was planning to return to the Church of England, Newman wrote in response:

> I do profess *ex animo*, with an absolute internal assent and consent, that Protestantism is the dreariest of possible religions; that the thought of the Anglican service makes me shiver, and the thought of the Thirty-nine Articles makes me shudder. Return to the Church of England! no; 'the net is broken, and we are delivered.' I should be a consummate fool (to use a mild term) if in my old age I left 'the land flowing with milk and honey' for the city of confusion and the house of bondage (*L.D.* xx, p. 216 [341]).

This letter, unsurprisingly, shocked and hurt his Anglican friends, typically Charles Crawley, a parishioner in Littlemore. He held Newman in high regard and they had continued to correspond. Newman explained to him that he had written in those harsh terms 'to force Protestants to put out of their minds the hope of my ever coming back to them' (*L.D.* xx, p. 236 [343]). He was exasperated by the constant rumours. His 1845 conversion had indeed been like coming into port after a rough sea. That did not mean, however, that thereafter everything had been tranquil and serene.

★

Newman was ordained a Catholic priest in Rome on 30 May 1847. The month before, between 8 and 17 April, he made a retreat, in preparation for his ordination. His notes from those days are revealing. He began, 'I have in my mind a wound or cancer, the presence of which prevents me from being a good Oratorian.' He describes himself as creeping along the ground, perhaps running, but unable to fly. His self-examination during these days was minutely searching.

He wrote that he found pleasure in going to Mass, in visits to the Blessed Sacrament, in saying the rosary and litanies and in reciting the Divine Office, but he confessed to being embarrassed by special devotions, such as the prayers to be said for gaining indulgences or within the nine days of a Novena. He commented, 'They overwhelm my memory, are a weight on my mind, distract and almost terrify me,' and added, 'all the more because I am perhaps liable to be scrupulous'.

Shortly afterwards, he looked back:

> When I was growing up, and as a young man, I had confidence and hope in God, i.e. I committed myself without anxiety to His Providence, I had the greatest faith in the efficacy of prayer, in all adversities I used to say calmly that He would deliver me and mine in His own good time.

However, reflecting at this point on events twenty years earlier, he recalled losing his 'natural and inborn faith'. Twenty years earlier takes us to the end of 1827 and the beginning of 1828 and so to his illness while examining at Oxford in the November, and then to the death of his sister Mary on 5 January. That crisis led him to take stock and may have helped to make his faith more mature. However, the loss of what he called his 'natural and inborn faith', his instinctive faith, he went on to say, made him 'much afraid of priesthood, lest I should behave without due reverence in something so sacred'. He recognised that he had remained affable and kind among his friends and other people, 'but gradually my original confidence in God's boundless love for me, and in the efficacy of my prayers has faded'. He continued:

> I have not lost either my intimate sense of the Divine Presence in every place, nor the good conscience and peace of mind that flows therefrom, but I no longer thought, or at any rate, much less than formerly, that the habit of prayer was not only a

83

prescribed duty but also a great talent and privilege, by which we can do all things.

By speaking of prayer as a talent he was not meaning a personal skill or achievement, but, as its link with privilege implies, rather as a gift, like the talents given to the servants by their master in the Gospel parable (Matthew 25:14–30). The habit of prayer was still a duty to be fulfilled, but no longer a gift exercised with much ease: 'That subtle and delicate vigour of faith has become dulled in me, and remains so to this day.'

It is important, therefore, not to underestimate how difficult the start of Newman's Catholic life was. These very personal notes seem to indicate almost a sense of bereavement. He felt disorientated. He was, as an Irish friend of mine once remarked, 'sideways'. He was feeling the loss of friends from his Anglican days and reacting against Catholic practices, such as fasts, meditations and retreats, which he 'did willingly in the Anglican Church'. He concluded, 'I am always languid in the contemplation of divine things, like a man walking with his feet bound together.' He described himself as having fallen into a kind of despair and a gloomy state of mind (*A.W.* pp. 245–8).

There is a further feature, however, which gives these retreat notes added significance. Many people have felt inspired by a particular passage from Newman's writings. The words are familiar:

> God has created me to do Him some definite service . . . I am a link in a chain, a bond of connexion between persons . . . Therefore I will trust Him. Whatever, wherever I am, I can never be thrown away. If I am in sickness, my sickness may serve Him; in perplexity, my perplexity may serve him; if I am in sorrow, my sorrow may serve Him. My sickness, or perplexity, or sorrow may be necessary causes of some great end, which is quite beyond us . . . still He knows what He is about (*M.D.* pp. 400–1).

These powerful words were published in *Meditations and Devotions* which came out, as we have noted, in 1893, three years after Newman's death, but they were actually composed on 8 March 1848, so within a year of those retreat notes in April 1847. However weighed down Newman may have felt, however dark the clouds gathering around him, he was resolved to be faithful, whether in sickness or perplexity or sorrow.

★

The clouds seem to have been darkest early in 1863. This was the time that Newman reflected on his situation at length in his journal. On 21 January, one sentence in particular seems to sum up his feeling:

> O how forlorn and dreary has been my course since I have been a Catholic! here has been the contrast – as a Protestant, I felt my religion dreary, but not my life – but as a Catholic, my life dreary, not my religion (*A.W.* p. 254).

As an Anglican, he had been living happily in Oxford and among many dear friends. Life was good. At that time, as we have seen, through the Tractarian Movement he had been struggling to restore to the Church of England its Catholic tradition which he felt had been lost. But, in spite of succeeding to a greater extent than he had perhaps anticipated, he then began to lose confidence in his championing of Anglicanism as a *via media* between error and excess, while the bishops' overwhelmingly negative response to *Tract 90* and their plan to establish the Jerusalem bishopric in collaboration with Lutherans and Calvinists signalled to him an Anglican alliance with Protestantism that he could not countenance.

Religion was dreary. Catholicism became, therefore, that coming into port: his decision had brought him 'perfect peace and contentment'. But life was another matter. The Catholic Church in 1845 was at a loss to know what to do with Newman.

What it did, in fact, was to invite him to undertake those various projects mentioned earlier: to found a university in Dublin; to oversee a fresh translation of the Bible; to edit that distinguished, though controversial, periodical *The Rambler*; and to establish an Oratory in Oxford to give pastoral care to the Catholic undergraduates who were by that time permitted to become members of that university. But each of these projects foundered through a combination of negligence, the incompetence of others, a lack of support, and sometimes even the hostility of those who had initially extended the invitations. Projects, of course, never emerge or falter of themselves. People propose or oppose them. Coincidentally, besides Newman, there were three key players in these projects, and they all became cardinals.

★

Nicholas Wiseman

Nicholas Wiseman became the first Cardinal Archbishop of Westminster in 1850, but Newman, as we have noticed already, had met him seventeen years earlier when he had visited him during his Mediterranean journey in 1833. At that time, Wiseman was the Rector of the English College in Rome. In 1840, however, he had been ordained as a coadjutor bishop to the Vicar Apostolic of the Central District and became President of Oscott, which was a school at that time, not a seminary. In that capacity he acquired responsibility for many of the new converts and was helpful to Newman. He refused, for example, to read Newman's *Essay on Development*; he wanted it to be read as written, without there being any possible suggestion that it had been censored. And it was Wiseman, we recall, when Newman went to Rome to discern his vocation and prepare for ordination as a Catholic priest, who suggested that he might become an Oratorian.

All that was good. Later, however, Newman remarked that, although he had not been clearly conscious of it at the time, he had felt humiliated at Oscott, disturbed by 'the gaze of so many eyes . . ., as if [I were] some wild incomprehensible beast, caught by the hunter, and a spectacle for Dr. Wiseman to exhibit to strangers, as himself being the hunter who captured it!' And he referred to having to stand outside Wiseman's door, 'waiting for Confession amid the Oscott boys' (*A.W.* p. 255). Here was a distinguished man in his mid-forties, having made a momentous decision by becoming a Catholic, being treated like a schoolboy.

Then, in 1851, when Giacinto Achilli, the former Dominican friar who had been convicted in Italy of sexual immorality, had been brought to England by the Evangelical Alliance to fuel anti-Catholic feeling, Newman denounced him in the fifth of his lectures on *The Present Position of Catholics in England*, exposing his immorality and hypocrisy. He felt confident in doing so because he used material that he had taken from a pamphlet written by Wiseman. Achilli, however, chose to sue Newman, not Wiseman, for libel. When Newman appealed to Wiseman for the evidence he needed, Wiseman had mislaid the vital papers.

Eventually, after many months, Newman was found guilty, as his charges were considered unproven. The judge's prejudiced handling of the case led Newman's counsel, the Attorney General Sir Alexander Cockburn, to ask for a retrial, which was denied. However, when Newman was sentenced, instead of being imprisoned, he was merely fined £100. Friends and supporters had already raised far more than that. But the whole sorry affair, which had dragged on for eighteen months, could have been avoided had Wiseman been less slow and disorganised.

Something similar happened in 1860. The previous year, having completed his term as Rector of the Catholic University in Dublin and returned to Birmingham, Newman was asked by his own bishop, Ullathorne, to rescue the periodical, *The Rambler*, from the danger of being attacked by some bishops in their pastoral letters. They were critical of the way *The Rambler* had criticised them, but the row would have caused a scandal. Newman as the new editor was seen as acceptable both to the bishops and to *The Rambler's* lay owners. It proved to be a painful experience. In a complex web of events he was regarded as too favourable towards the laity so that in the end he only edited two issues. But he took the opportunity in the second to write an article explaining his view on consulting the faithful in doctrinal matters. His view was not well received by some in high places and a complaint was dispatched to Rome.

What part did Wiseman play in this episode?

To deal with the complaint, Newman was advised to contact Wiseman because he was on the spot in Rome at the time. Newman wrote him a letter on 19 January 1860, asking which passages in the article were thought to require explanation. He also asked for a copy of the translation of his article that had been read and to be told which dogmatic propositions the passages had been represented as infringing or impairing. He promised his wholehearted acceptance of the dogmatic propositions, to explain the article in accordance with them and to show that the English text and the content of the article were consistent with the propositions (*L.D.* xix. pp. 289–90 [325–6]).

Wiseman received this letter and forwarded it to the Congregation of Propaganda, which had received the complaint. Statements were drawn up, as Newman had requested, and were returned to Wiseman on 30 January, but after that nothing happened. Again, Wiseman was disorganised and, to be fair, was also becoming unwell. The matter was supposed to be resolved on his return to England, but Newman heard nothing further and assumed everything was settled. Propaganda, on the other hand, having received no reply from Newman, regarded him as recalcitrant or disobedient.

Seven years later, when Newman's friend Ambrose St John was in Rome on another matter altogether, he discovered that Newman was still viewed unfavourably for his failure to reply. St John, however, was able to show a copy of Newman's letter to Wiseman to Cardinal Alessandro Barnabò, the Prefect of Propaganda. Barnabò was astonished. 'Why, Cardinal Wiseman was at Propaganda,' he exclaimed, 'and we never heard of this.' And so the matter was finally closed.[1]

Other examples of Wiseman's lack of consideration for Newman could be mentioned. In 1855 he proposed dedicating jointly to Newman and Frederick Faber a panegyric on St Philip Neri. It was a proposal, because of tensions between himself and Faber, that Newman judged to be inappropriate. He agreed on the condition that he was not to be singled out, but the Birmingham Fathers were to be included. Wiseman carried on regardless.

Then, in 1857, Wiseman invited Newman to oversee that fresh translation of the Bible. But the invitation evaporated because of Wiseman's failure to carry through what he had begun, leaving Newman with costs and the need to explain his inaction to the American bishops with whom he found he was supposed to be collaborating. The Americans were understanding.

After Wiseman's death, Newman commented to his Irish friend Charles Russell that, while Wiseman had done a great work, notably in restoring the Catholic Hierarchy of the Bishops of England and Wales, he personally had 'not much to thank him for, since I was a Catholic'. He explained, 'He always meant kindly, but his impulses, kind as they were, were evanescent, and he was naturally influenced by those who got around him and occupied his ear' (*L.D.* xxi, p. 426 [385]).

---

1 For a fuller account, see Roderick Strange, 'Newman on Consulting the Faithful: Context, Content, and Consequences', *New Blackfriars* 98 (March 2017), pp. 134–46.

Paul Cullen

In April 1851, months before the storm surrounding Achilli was about to break, Newman received a letter from Archbishop Paul Cullen of Armagh, inquiring whether Newman could recommend someone to be the Superior of the university that the Irish bishops had decided to establish in Dublin. He also asked whether Newman might come over and deliver some lectures on education. By the July, Newman had himself been appointed Rector, and the following year he delivered the lectures that became the core of his major work, *The Idea of a University*.

For the next seven years Newman travelled regularly between Dublin and Birmingham. For the first three years he must have felt as though he was treading water: events moved very slowly, as the university was not opened formally until 1854. He must have felt anxious at the same time, because his trial for libelling Achilli was taking place during much of that period. In the mid-fifties as well he clashed with Frederick Faber, the Superior of the London Oratory, over the interpretation of their Oratorian Rule. A painful, futile dispute erupted between the Birmingham and Brompton Oratories, which was not to be healed for decades.[2] That was the backcloth to a stressful time.

What made matters particularly trying for Newman, however, was Paul Cullen's behaviour. Newman could not get him to make decisions. When he did make them, he did so without consulting Newman. An outstanding example was the appointment of a Vice Rector. Newman wanted to make the appointment himself. As the Vice Rector would at times be his representative, he wanted that person to be someone with whom he could work. But he did not want to rush. He needed time so as to make the appointment when he knew the likely

2 See chapter 8, p. 107.

candidates better. His request was ignored. And the man Cullen chose, Patrick Leahy, though admirable and in sympathy with Newman, was appointed, as Newman observed later, to represent the Irish Archbishops 'as their safeguard and security against me, [rather] than as my own helper and backer up' (*A.W.* p. 294).

Then, when the university church that Newman had had built in St Stephen's Green was, in spite of some financial wrangling with Cullen, just ready for opening, Cullen wrote to Newman to ask a series of questions about the length of the lease, an issue that could have prevented the church's consecration, about the priests who would officiate there, about who would own it were Newman to leave, and about who would preach there. Newman replied, acknowledging the letter. Then followed two terse sentences: 'I am very glad to have elicited your Grace's questions. I should have been still more gratified to have elicited them some time ago; but your Grace is the judge whether they could have been asked at an earlier date' (*L.D.* xvii, p. 212 [295]).

On 1 February 1857, Newman wrote a letter to John Capes that sums up his 'personal annoyance' at the way Cullen treated him. His exasperation is unmistakable:

I will tell you his *rule* of acting – not once or twice, but his rule and principle – to let me ask a question in June, to call about it again and again, to let me write to him about it in July, to let me write to his intimate friend to get an answer for me in August, to give up the chance of one in September, and in January accidentally to find he all along has been telling others that he *has* decided it in the way I asked him *not* to decide in, though even now in February he has not, directly or indirectly, answered me. I say, this is his way of doing business – and the sort of confidence he places in *me* (*L.D.* xvii, p. 514 [302]).

And he observed to another friend, 'He has treated me from the first like a scrub' (*L.D.* xviii, p. 487).

In spite of the tensions and difficulties between them, however, Cullen, who was made a cardinal in 1866, spoke well of Newman in later years. When Newman was criticised in Rome for the position he had taken on the temporal power of the papacy, Cullen supported him, and when there were those in Rome keen to criticise the account he had given of papal infallibility in his *Letter to the Duke of Norfolk*, Cullen praised it in a pastoral letter. His voice, with others, silenced the criticism.

Henry Manning

One of the others was Henry Manning. The *Letter* had been received so well in England that he realised that any breath of disapproval would do more harm than good. Yet Manning and Newman are commonly viewed as being deeply at odds with each other. The truth is less straightforward.

Both had been Anglicans; both had been ordained Anglican priests; both were fellows of Oxford colleges, Newman at Oriel and Manning at Merton; both were involved in the Tractarian Movement; both became Catholics, Newman in 1845 and Manning in 1851; and both became Catholic priests and, later, cardinals. Although it is true that they were never close friends, they had certainly been friendly. Much of their correspondence bears witness to that. As an Anglican, Manning had been married. When his wife, Caroline, was dying in 1837, Newman wrote to comfort him. The day after her death, Manning thanked him: 'I hardly know what has drawn me so closely, and in one way suddenly to your sympathy, but I feel something in the way you deal with my sorrows, particularly soothing and strengthening' (*L.D.* vi, p. 102, n. 1 [105]).

Much later, in 1862, at the Oratory School that Newman had founded, there was a crisis that could have led to its collapse: almost the entire teaching staff seemed about to resign. Manning wrote to Newman from Rome, expressing his support, wanting him to know 'that I share in anything that pains you' (*L.D.* xx. p. 133, n. 2 [337]). And four years later, after hearing that Keble had died, he told Newman, 'I feel as if it had put me back half my life to the days when we used to look to him and his Christian Year as the service of our happiest thoughts. Nobody can understand this as you, and I write to you almost instinctively' (*L.D.* xxii, p. 198 [404]). They were not always at loggerheads.

Nevertheless, three issues in particular divided them. First, there was the question of the pope's temporal power. By the time the drive for the unification of Italy with the exception of the Papal States came to be achieved in 1860, Manning had become its passionate advocate. Newman's view was more detached. As he told a friend, Thomas Allies, in 1866, 'though I have no difficulty in saying that the temporal power is necessary, while it lasts, nothing can make me say it is necessary, if it be clean taken away'. He added, 'I am quite as sure that, when it is clean gone, if that ever took place, no Pope would say that it was necessary, as I am sure no Pope will say that Our Lord is a mere man' (*L.D.* xxii, p. 303 [411]).

Second, hand in hand with his passion for the pope's temporal power, Manning championed an extreme interpretation of papal infallibility, whereas Newman did not. With troops marching on Rome, Manning was a leader of those who urged the bishops at the First Vatican Council to define the doctrine as dogma. In a confidential letter to his bishop, which soon became well known, Newman protested, 'When has definition of doctrine de fide been a luxury of devotion, and not a stern painful necessity? Why should an aggressive insolent faction be allowed to "make the heart of the just mourn, whom the Lord hath not made sorrowful?"' (*L.D.* xxv, pp. 18–19 [442]).

The third issue on which they disagreed was university education. Changes at Oxford in 1854 had made it possible for those who were not members of the Church of England to matriculate. On two occasions in the 1860s, Newman was encouraged by his bishop, Ullathorne, to open a mission in Oxford to care for the Catholics who might attend the university. On both occasions the attempt failed. The bishops in general and Manning in particular, by now a bishop himself, were implacably opposed to such a move, on the grounds that an Oxford education would weaken the young Catholics' hold on their faith. But Newman's involvement was also a vital factor. Indeed, in 1867, the second attempt was finally abandoned when Newman discovered that the permission that he had received from Rome for the enterprise included a secret clause to prevent his actually residing.

Newman was not surprised. He had suspected such a manoeuvre. Some years earlier he had heard from his friend, the lawyer Edward Bellasis, who had been visiting Rome, that Manning was more opposed to him going to Oxford than to Catholic youth going there (see *L.D.* xxii, pp. 328–9 [414]). When he informed Ullathorne that he was declining formally his invitation to open the mission, Ullathorne, in acknowledging his letter, observed, 'I have no hesitation in saying it, as my complete conviction that you have been shamefully misrepresented at Rome, and that by countrymen of our own' (*L.D.* xxiii, p. 312, n. 2 [427]). He was not referring only to Manning, but Manning would have been included in that judgment.

Manning had become suspicious of Newman. Part of Newman's genius is to be seen in the way, as he moved forward, faithful to the gospel, entering ever more deeply into the life of the Church, he was able to preserve what was good and valuable from his past. Manning cherished his past as well, but he saw in Newman, as we noticed earlier, the 'danger of an English Catholicism of which Newman is the highest type'. He described him as worldly and his work as 'the old Anglican, patristic, literary Oxford tone transplanted into the Church. It takes the line', he went on, 'of deprecating exaggerations, foreign devotions, Ultramontanism, anti-national sympathies.'[3] So it is hardly surprising that, when the possibility arose in 1879 of making Newman a cardinal, the idea would not have been welcome to Manning.

In those days, however, cardinals who were not diocesan bishops virtually always resided in Rome. Newman felt honoured by the invitation but knew that he was too old to move. How could he accept and still remain in Birmingham? To suggest such an outcome would have seemed like bargaining with the pope. Bishop Ullathorne, enthused by the prospect, suggested a solution. He advised Newman to write, expressing his gratitude but also explaining how impossible it would be for him to move from his Oratory to Rome. On the face of it, he might appear to be declining the offer. But to accompany it Ullathorne would write a covering letter, explaining the situation and expressing Newman's actual acceptance. He was confident that the pope had no intention of requiring Newman to move from his home.

Both letters were sent to Manning to take to Rome. A chance remark of Manning's, however, led Ullathorne to suspect that he would pass on the letter Newman had written – the one apparently refusing the offer – without the accompanying explanation. Manning, while travelling to Rome, even let slip that Newman had refused. When the news broke, there was uproar. Realising his mistake, Manning was quick to set matters right.

People have often questioned Manning's motives in this episode. Was he being devious? Or perhaps, given their contrasting views, was the wish that Newman would decline father to the thought? David Newsome has spoken of Manning's desire to win people over to his side, rather than truly wanting

3 See Newsome, *The Convert Cardinals*, p. 257.

to meet them halfway.[4] Newman was having none of it. He was not going to let himself be manipulated. As he once told Manning, 'I do not know whether I am on my head or my heels when I have active relations with you. In spite of my friendly feelings, this is the judgment of my intellect' (*L.D.* xxiv, pp. 362–3 [435]). The closer friendship of earlier years had ended. Once the matter of the cardinalate was settled, however, he was adamant in his defence of Manning. He told one correspondent:

> I wish to give a contradiction to any ideas that may be afloat as to any dissatisfaction on my part with any step taken by Cardinal Manning. He has been kind enough to go out of his way to write to me, and I wish every such report swept away for good and all (*L.D.* xxix, p. 76).

★

Many of those early years of Newman's Catholic life, about which he wrote in that journal entry in January 1863, were cloudy and dark. His difficulties cannot all be laid at the feet of Wiseman, Cullen and Manning. He was not always easy to deal with. But those relationships, in each of which there was also goodness and kindness, illustrate the challenges he had to face that could, as he said, make life 'dreary'. In some ways, in 1863 the difficulties with Manning were only just beginning.

All the same, if these key figures created hardship for Newman, over the years there grew between himself and his own bishop, William Bernard Ullathorne, a deepening respect and appreciation. Their relationship had not always been easy either. The part Ullathorne played in *The Rambler* affair, for example, and then in encouraging Newman's attempts to begin a mission in Oxford, was more complex than may appear from this brief account. But, as old men, each had a sense of

4 Newsome, *The Convert Cardinals*, p. 371.

the worth of the other. In 1887 the old bishop visited the aged
cardinal. When he was leaving, Newman sank to his knees and
asked for his blessing. Ullathorne was taken aback, but felt he
could not refuse. He did not want to embarrass Newman. He
did as he was asked. Newman told him, 'I have been indoors
all my life, whilst you have battled for the Church in the world.'
Relating the incident, Ullathorne observed, 'I felt annihilated
in his presence: there is a saint in that man.'[5]

5 Quoted in Gilley, *Newman in His Age*, p. 419.

8

Pastoral ministry[1]

'I have been indoors all my life.' Newman's words to his bishop, Ullathorne, seem to reinforce the stereotype of him as a reclusive intellectual, the writer of famous books, far removed from the demands of ordinary, everyday life. Yet what we have already considered suggests a different picture. There was his leadership of the Oxford Movement during his Anglican days with all that that involved, and then, as a Catholic, as well as establishing the Oratories in Birmingham and London, the series of projects he was invited to undertake: the founding of the university in Dublin, preparing oversight of a fresh translation of the Bible, editing *The Rambler* and, on two occasions, making plans to set up a mission in Oxford for the Catholic youth who might go there. These projects were time consuming and, although they may have been thwarted, that was never because Newman had been incompetent. And it would also be a mistake to forget that what he wrote was not a series of lofty, abstract tomes, but was written in response to need. The great commandment instructs us to love our neighbour as well as God. Even hermits and monks and nuns with vocations to enclosed religious life must never despise or neglect the world. Ullathorne had indeed been battling in the world

1 Some material in this chapter, used with permission, is adapted from an article of mine that appeared in *New Blackfriars* (March 2011), pp. 255–63.

all his life, but, in his own way, Newman had been battling there too. His pastoral instinct was evident very early on.

★

We have seen that Newman's early earnest, evangelical conversion in 1816 was unmistakably significant for him. By the time he was elected a fellow of Oriel, its intensity may have lessened, but still he felt its influence. He was ordained as an Anglican deacon on 13 June 1824 and he recorded the occasion in his journal: 'It is over. I am thine, O Lord; I seem quite dizzy, and cannot altogether believe and understand it. At first, after the hands were laid on me, my heart shuddered within me; the words "for ever" are so terrible' (*A.W.* p. 200). The intensity of his emotion is unmistakable.

The following year, on 29 May, he was ordained as an Anglican priest. During the time between these two ordinations he worked in the Oxford parish of St Clement's in Cowley, just over Magdalen Bridge. Again, there is an entry in his journal where he reflected on the way he had changed since he had become a deacon. 'Then,' he wrote, 'I thought the *onus probandi* lay with those who asserted an individual to be a real Christian; and now I think it lies with those who deny it.' As an earnest evangelical he had felt that there needed to be proof when someone was claimed to be a genuine Christian; now, however, he had come to think that the claim should be accepted, unless there was clear proof to the contrary. He admitted he was still not convinced about baptismal regeneration, that 'the Spirit always or generally accompanies the very act of baptism', but his position had shifted.

Some weeks later, on 17 July, he explained the change. 'I have been principally or in great measure led to this change', he observed, 'by the fact that in my parochial duties I found many, who in most important points were inconsistent, but whom I could not say were altogether without grace' (*A.W.* p. 206). What had made the difference? The people, his parishioners themselves. Theoretical theology had been qualified by pastoral practice. His pastoral instinct had been stirred.

★

The instinct next found expression most obviously in his approach to his responsibilities as a tutor. He was convinced that students flourished, not so much from general lectures as from the individual guidance a tutor could supply. In the course of a lengthy correspondence with Provost Hawkins at Oriel, he explained that he knew 'by experience . . . the mere lecturing required of me would be incompatible with due attention to that more useful private instruction, which has imparted to the office of Tutor the importance of a clerical occupation' (*L.D.* ii, p. 233 [45]).

General lecturing impeded effective tutoring. And he linked private tutoring to the clerical state, his priestly vocation. He saw personal influence as positive, not manipulative, and as an essential part of a tutor's role. One of his university sermons, preached in 1832, was called, 'Personal Influence, the Means of Propagating the Truth' (*U.S.* pp. 75–98 [62–77]). And more than twenty years later in Dublin he was to make the same point in stirring words that have been quoted often: 'An academical system without the personal influence of teachers upon pupils, is an arctic system; it will create an ice-bound, petrified, cast-iron University, and nothing else' (*H.S.* iii, p. 74).

But, as we know, Hawkins was unconvinced. He preferred the established way. Newman lost the argument and gradually had no further pupils appointed to him.

★

After 1833, however, Newman was absorbed by the Oxford Movement, writing tracts and distributing them, and, of course, as vicar of St Mary the Virgin, preaching the sermons that have so often been acclaimed. Then by 1835 he had another concern, the building of the church in Littlemore.

The parishioners there felt they needed a church of their own. On 31 May Newman preached a sermon in St Mary's, supporting them and appealing on their behalf. We have noticed this sermon already, when exploring Newman's growing awareness of the significance of the Lord's presence in the Eucharist. Later in that sermon, he read out part of the address that the people from Littlemore had composed. They had written, 'Each year we feel more and more the want of a Church, our distance from St Mary's makes it impossible for us to attend and the neighbouring Churches are barely sufficient for their own parishioners.' The address went on to detail the consequences, such as people rarely attending church at all, or having to go to dissenting chapels and even being buried from them, while fearing that their 'children and neighbours should come to lose their attachment to those ordinances they ought most highly to esteem'.[2]

The address Newman was reading had been sent to the Governing Body at Oriel. They had received it most favourably, made a donation of £100 and provided a plot of land. By the following year the church had been built.

Littlemore, of course, was a place Newman came to love dearly. We return to old ground. He retired to live there in 1842, agonised over his position in the Church of England there, preached 'The Parting of Friends', his final Anglican sermon there, and wrote there his *Essay on Development*. He had been received as a Catholic there, as we know, and remained there till 1846, when, with great emotion, he tore himself away.

He returned twice. He visited with Ambrose St John on a hot day in June 1868. They went from Birmingham and back within the day, and spent five hours walking around and meeting people. He told William Copeland, who had been his curate, 'I wanted to see it once more before I died . . . I rejoiced to see

2 Ms. Sermon, no 388, McGrath (ed.), *John Henry Newman: Sermons 1824–1843*, iv, p. 95.

Littlemore so green.' He also told him, 'We saw Mrs Palmer, young Humphries and his second wife (a Boswell) – old Mrs Humphries and her daughter – Martha King – Charles Pollard's nephew – Mr Whitlock', parishioners whom he remembered (*L.D.* xxiv, pp. 94–5 [432]). His priestly care for Littlemore had meant much to him. And he went again, ten years later, on 10 September 1878. This time he went alone and visited his mother's garden and was 'amazed how beautiful 40 years had made it'. Then the owner came out, he told his friend Anne Mozley, 'took me in and gave me a glass of sherry' (*L.D.* xxviii, pp. 400, 410–11). He was obviously made welcome.

In 1840, however, he was already wondering about resigning St Mary's. In a letter to Keble, he acknowledged that initiatives he had taken had made their mark, but he felt he was 'converting a parochial charge into a sort of University office'. He began by lamenting, 'It is certain that I do not know my Oxford Parishioners; I am not conscious of influencing them; and certainly I have no insight into their spiritual state' (*L.D.* vii, p. 416 [126]). He seemed to himself to be failing pastorally. But Keble managed to persuade him to stay, and it was to be another three years before finally he resigned.

★

Newman may have felt out of touch with his parishioners at St Mary's, but all the same it was his parochial preaching that made his years as vicar so memorable. We have already noted Owen Chadwick's remark that it was of the essence of the Oxford Movement 'that its best writing should be enshrined in [Newman's] parochial sermons'.[3] However, when the first volume of those sermons appeared, it was criticised for concentrating on some points and neglecting others, for concentrating on failure and arousing people's fears, for threatening them without offering them comfort.

3 Chadwick, *The Mind of the Oxford Movement*, p. 42.

Newman was unmoved by the criticism. He felt that something stern was needed to counter a general disposition that had grown slack. He was responding to a need. He informed Samuel Wilberforce, who had been one of the first to express this criticism, 'I lay it down as a fundamental Canon, that a Sermon to be effective must be imperfect.' What a comfort for those of us required to preach regularly! He was not encouraging poor preaching, but making a vital pastoral point. Who has not heard sermons that are overlong because the preacher has tried to say too much, to include everything? Good preachers highlight one point on one occasion, another on another, contemplating the mystery. Those unpublished 1836 sermons on Christ offer a prime example of his method, moving from one aspect of the mystery to another: Christ's unity, his divinity, and his humanity. And Newman remarked to Wilberforce, 'No one, who *habitually* hears me, ought to have any other than the whole Scripture impression' (*L.D.* v, p. 38 [85]). That was in 1835.

More than thirty years later, on 2 March 1868, Newman gave a detailed answer to a student from Maynooth who asked his advice about preaching (see *L.D.* xxiv, pp. 44–5 [428–9]). Wilfrid Ward published the notes Newman prepared for his reply in his biography. They remain fascinating:

1 'A man should be in earnest, by which I mean he should write not for the sake of writing, but to bring out his thoughts.' We might say: when preaching, be yourself. I remember being told always to believe what I was saying when preaching.

2 'He should never aim at being eloquent.' It is a warning against being artificial or fancy; people detect what does not ring true.

3 'He should keep his idea in view, and should write sentences over and over again till he has expressed his meaning accurately, forcibly, and in a few words.' This anticipates what he was to say to John Hayes in Shropshire the following year,

where he also acknowledged Cicero as the only master of style he had ever had. In his actual letter to this student he was specific: 'Take care it should be one subject, not several.' It is important to be clear and keep just one subject in view.

4 'He should aim at being understood by his hearers or readers.'

5 'He should use words which are likely to be understood. Ornament and amplification will come spontaneously in due time, but he should never seek them.' Both these points are emphasising the importance of being intelligible. That may seem too obvious to need saying, but how often what people say in public is convoluted and baffling.

6 'He must creep before he can fly, by which I mean that humility which is a great Christian virtue, has a place in literary composition.' In other words, we might say, keep it simple.

7 'He who is ambitious will never write well, but he who tries to say simply what he feels, what religion demands, what faith teaches, what the Gospel promises, will be eloquent without intending, and will write better English than if he made a study of English literature.'[4]

The pastoral heart, the pastoral instinct, is evident in these guidelines.

*

These reflections relate largely to the time of Newman's Anglican Ministry. What happened after 1845?

At the start there was an almost comical contrast. We remember Newman's intensity and earnestness when he was ordained as an Anglican deacon. However, when he was ordained a Catholic priest on 30 May 1847, he sent a letter later that day to Elizabeth Bowden. 'You will be pleased to

4 Ward, *The Life of John Henry Cardinal Newman* ii, pp. 335–6.

hear', he told her, 'I was ordained Priest about two hours ago; surprised, perhaps, for things have progressed so rapidly that I do not know what I said in my last letter' (*L.D.* xii, p. 84 [230]). While it is not always easy to catch the tone of written remarks, there seems to be an unmistakable air of slightly amused bewilderment here, very different from those earnest words in 1824.

After his ordination, Newman entered the Oratorian novitiate in Rome and then returned to England in time for Christmas to set up the English Oratory. By February 1848 he had been joined by Frederick Faber and his group of Wilfridians, as they had been known (because, through an agreement with the Earl of Shrewsbury, they had acquired responsibility for St Wilfrid's, Cotton). Shrewsbury expected the Oratorians to continue fulfilling the obligations the Wilfridians had undertaken. He had envisaged a community living there. But Cotton was countryside, while the Oratorian mission was focused on cities.

Faber, once an Oratorian, rather ignored the dilemma that St Wilfrid's created, and it was Newman who gradually had to disentangle them, while continuing to care for St Wilfrid's until another community could be found. Some Passionists moved in at the end of 1850. Before then, Newman had even brought all the Oratorians there for some months, from October 1848 until the opening of the Oratory in Alcester Street in Birmingham the following February. From that time, therefore, for virtually two years, from February 1849 until the end of 1850, he was overseeing the pastoral needs at St Wilfrid's from Birmingham.

The Oratorians moved from Alcester Street to their permanent home in Edgbaston in February 1852. A house in London was opened some months later. These early Catholic years were plainly packed with practical and pastoral activity. And from the autumn of 1851, of course, the Achilli trial was looming, while plans were beginning to take shape for founding the university in Dublin.

Although he travelled back from Dublin quite frequently and remained in close touch with the community by letter, Newman's absence in Ireland obviously kept him at a distance from daily pastoral duties in Birmingham. It was during these years that the painful dispute erupted between his own Oratory and the London House. The Fathers at Brompton wished for a dispensation to undertake the spiritual care of nuns – something that had not been envisaged in the Oratorian Rule adapted for England and drawn up by Newman. All could have been well because the different Oratories were independent; but, without informing Newman, they asked for an interpretation of the Rule from Rome, and a formal ruling could have had implications for Birmingham as well.

When Newman discovered what had happened, he wrote to London, asking them to rectify the situation with Rome by writing a letter that he, as the person who had brought the English Rule to England, would transmit to the Congregation of Propaganda. But the London Fathers felt he was being high-handed and authoritarian. Matters deteriorated. Underlying it all was the clash of personalities between Newman, based contentedly and inconspicuously in Birmingham, and Faber, flamboyant and excitable and enjoying the London limelight. Affectionate letters were exchanged, but, as the Londoners failed to acknowledge that they had acted mistakenly and threatened the Rule, Newman was not appeased. Early in 1856 he took the time to go to Rome to ensure the independence of the English Oratories from each other. His suspicion of Faber grew and would never be overcome. The breakdown in relations between the two Oratories lasted for years. While Newman is generally recognised as having been in the right, this episode does not show him in the best light. He could be implacable.

Pastoral ministry creates pressures of its own. It is not hard to find examples. Naturally enough, after his return to Birmingham, Newman became involved in the Oratory parish once again. When, however, in 1862, Stanislas Flanagan decided amicably to leave the community and return to parish life in Ireland, we find Newman writing to Ambrose St John, asking him who would be available to hear confessions: 'If you give up confessions (as you must),[5] I shall be the only one left, shall I not?' (see *L.D.* xx, p. 261).

Then there was the famous occasion in 1864, after he had written the *Apologia* and when he was beginning once more to be held in high regard, when Monsignor George Talbot sent him a pompous letter, inviting him to preach in Rome, 'where you would have a more educated audience of Protestants than could ever be the case in England'. Newman's reply was curt and crisp. 'Birmingham people have souls,' he reminded Talbot, 'and I have neither taste nor talent for the sort of work you cut out for me: and I beg to decline your offer' (*L.D.* xxi, pp. 166–7 [374]).

Newman loved Birmingham and its people. By the time he died, it has been noted that his 'years of quiet, unassuming pastoral work – visiting the housebound, finding jobs for the unemployed, giving coal to the poor, paying for medicines for the sick, hearing confessions, preaching and saying mass, his enormous correspondence – had left their mark'.[6] Indeed, even in great old age, in November 1889, he went out in the snow to visit the Quakers, George Cadbury and his brother, to ask them to allow the Catholic girls who worked for them not to attend the daily Bible instruction with the other girls, but to say their own prayers in another room. The brothers were charmed by him and so the matter was settled. Cardinal Vincent Nichols remarked, once the news broke that Newman

---

5 Ambrose St John had become the headmaster of the Oratory School that Newman had founded in 1859, following the resignation, as we shall see below, of Nicholas Darnell in 1861.

6 Paul Chavasse, 'Newman and Birmingham', in Lefebvre and Mason (eds), *John Henry Newman in His Time*, p. 97.

was to be canonised, 'For me the truly remarkable nature of this moment is that this is an English parish priest being declared a saint.'[7]

★

If Newman's life in the 1850s was largely absorbed by his commitments in Dublin, reviewing his pastoral ministry in the 1860s offers a further, instructive perspective. Recall the events of those years: the consequences of his article about consulting the faithful continued to rumble on and he felt worn down by his sense of personal failure; in 1864 there was his dispute with Charles Kingsley that led him to write his *Apologia pro Vita Sua*; on two occasions, the first in 1864 and then again in 1867, there were the negotiations amid uncertainty about whether or not he should found an Oratory in Oxford; in 1865 he composed *The Dream of Gerontius*, and later that year he became involved in that debate about Marian doctrine and devotion with his friend, Edward Pusey; then in 1866 he at last became clear about how to tackle a book he had long wanted to write, which became *A Grammar of Assent* and was published in 1870. During those years as well the summoning of the First Vatican Council was announced, triggering controversy and anxiety about whether papal infallibility would be defined as a dogma and, if so, the terms in which the definition would be couched. With regard to his correspondence, there are five and a half large published volumes of letters for this decade alone. Plenty was happening. And at the same time, as well as his care for the parish, there was his increased responsibility for the Oratory School.

He had founded the School very soon after his return from Dublin, and had appointed Father Nicholas Darnell as head-master. Darnell was gifted and a strict disciplinarian, although Newman came to believe that he was too fond of corporal

7 Statement on the Westminster Diocese website, 12 February 2019.

punishment. Before long, Darnell sought to have complete control, wishing to make the school virtually independent of the Oratory. He was particularly averse to the influence of Frances Wootten, the Matron, who was a widow, a convert and a friend of Newman's. He resented her care of the younger boys. Newman stood firm. So, before Christmas 1861, Darnell and the four other members of staff resigned. The school's very existence was threatened. Over the holiday period, however, the crisis was resolved. Some of the staff apologised and were re-employed, and other teachers were found. Ambrose St John took over as headmaster.[8]

The famous public schools at the time had a high academic reputation, but they were largely unconcerned with the moral and spiritual welfare of their pupils. (That began to change at Arnold's Rugby.) By contrast, Catholic schools, like Stonyhurst, Downside and Oscott, were stronger on moral and spiritual welfare but weaker academically. Newman, bearing in mind those families who had become Catholic and wanted a Catholic education for their sons, but wanted as well an education to match the academic standard that would have been available at schools like Eton and Harrow, founded the Oratory School to combine the academic quality of those public schools with the moral and spiritual care that was more characteristic of their Catholic counterparts.[9] Once again, pastoral concern was crucial for him. What he had championed as a tutor at Oriel and affirmed in Dublin was guiding him still.

★

When we survey Newman's life, as newly ordained, as a College tutor, as a preacher and as a parish priest, his pastoral instinct is unmistakable. It was evident as well, as we have seen,

8 See Gilley, *Newman and His Age*, pp. 312–3.
9 See Paul Shrimpton, *A Catholic Eton? Newman's Oratory School* (Leominster: Gracewing, 2005).

in his care for navigating a middle way between error and excess and in his approach to education. As an occasional writer, he wrote in response to need. That inclination too was pastoral. Even his *Essay in Aid of a Grammar of Assent*, often mentioned as the one exception to his occasional writings in the Newman corpus, was deeply and intentionally pastoral, inspired by his concern to show how the Gospel mysteries come alive and are made real for us.

A pastoral disposition involves relationships: relationships with oneself, with God and with others, which brings us back once more to the young John Henry Newman, just fifteen years of age, convinced, even were he to doubt everything else, of the existence of 'two and two only absolute and luminously self-evident beings': himself and his Creator (*Apo*. p. 4 [18]). It offers a kind of snapshot: he knew himself and he was convinced of the reality of God. And then, as a young Anglican deacon, he soon discovered grace in his first parishioners; he was learning from his relationships with them. The foundation of his pastoral instinct had been laid. Here was the beginning of the man who in 1870 would declare that he had no truck with 'smart syllogisms' for winning converts because he did 'not care to overcome [people's] reason without touching their hearts' (*G.A.* p. 425 [273]).

Newman was a pastor from the depths of his innermost heart to the pen at his fingertips.

9

A talent for educating

In August 1889 London became paralysed by a dock strike. The dockers were demanding sixpence an hour instead of the fourpence or even threepence they were being paid. For a month, the city was in turmoil. Cardinal Manning was appalled by the chaos and sympathetic to the dockers' demand. At one stage the owners agreed that their demand was to be met, but not until 1 January. The dockers, however, insisted that the agreement should begin on 4 September. So the deadlock continued.

Although eighty-one years of age and increasingly frail, Manning was determined to do what he could to resolve the crisis. He attended meetings, persisted in negotiating and, finally, on 10 September, went alone to a long meeting with the committee of strike leaders. When, late in the day, still no agreement was in sight, he spoke passionately, pleading with them to accept that he was impartial and to recognise the danger to the nation and the suffering they could bring upon their own families if the strike dragged on. In spite of some diehard resistance, the meeting finally accepted his proposed compromise date of 4 November and authorised him to negotiate a settlement with the Joint Committee on those terms. The strike was as good as over and Manning was hailed in the press as the hero of the hour.[1]

1 See Robert Gray, *Cardinal Manning: A Biography* (London: Weidenfeld & Nicolson, 1985), pp. 306–9.

Among those who congratulated him was Newman. In reply, Manning wrote, 'Your letter this morning is as grateful to me, as it was unlooked for: and I thank you for it very heartily' (*L.D.* xxxi, p. 276, n. 3). There was nothing in Newman's life that compared with Manning's triumph in bringing the dock strike to an end. But talents vary.

In St Matthew's Gospel (Matthew 25:14–30), Jesus tells a parable about a man going on a journey who distributes talents to his servants, five to one, two to another, and just one to a third. The man who receives just the one is cautious and goes and buries it to keep it safe. When the master returns, the servant is punished for his idleness. But it is the master's reaction to the other two that is instructive. The servant given five talents has made five more, and the servant given two has made two more, but here is the point: both are praised equally. A telling lesson of the parable is to set aside any hierarchy in giftedness. Some people are gifted in one way; others in another. The crucial question asks not what gifts they have or which are superior, but how their gifts have been used. Manning became a champion of social Catholicism; Newman had a talent for educating.

★

From the very start, Newman was devoted to education. His life was studded with particular projects. As we have seen, he began as a tutor at Oriel. By the time his understanding of the way that office should be fulfilled had been rejected and no more pupils were allotted to him, he had become the vicar of the university church, St Mary the Virgin. There, besides his parochial sermons, filled with their memorable catechetical power, he delivered in the Adam de Brome Chapel two notable series of lectures, one on the prophetical office and the other on justification.

He was always seeking to educate, to help people be better informed. Later there were his seven years as Rector of the

university in Dublin and, afterwards, on his return, his founding of the Oratory School. Then, as we have noted, at his
bishop's request, he attempted twice in the 1860s to establish a
mission in Oxford for the Catholics who might be going to
the university. But it was not only a matter of particular
projects.

In that long entry in his journal on 21 January 1863, when
everything he touched seemed destined to fail, he made a
statement that came straight from the heart. He wrote:

> Catholics in England, from their very blindness, cannot see
> that they are blind. To aim then at improving the condition,
> the status, of the Catholic body, by a careful survey of their
> argumentative basis, of their position relatively to the philoso-
> phy and the character of the day, by giving them juster views,
> by enlarging and refining their minds, in one word, by educa-
> tion, is (in their view) more than a superfluity or a hobby, it is
> an insult. It implies that they are deficient in material points.
> Now from first to last, education, in this large sense of the
> word, has been my line . . . (*A.W.* p. 259).

The note of exasperation is unmistakable: Catholics are so
blind they cannot see they are blind. So he emphasised the
importance of supplying them with better arguments to help
them make their case more effectively, of making them more
alert to contemporary culture, 'the philosophy and the character of the day', of establishing a better base, 'giving them juster
views', and of broadening and deepening their understanding.
That was his objective, not just education, but education, as he
observed, in the 'large sense of the word': that was his line.

What exasperated him, however, also makes me smile to
myself. Having been to a Jesuit school, I have often been asked
why I did not become a Jesuit. My stock reply has been that I
did not want to become a teacher, as so many Jesuits were in
those days fifty years or more ago. I smile because, since my

return from Rome in 1970, I have always been involved in education in one way or another. First of all there was my doctoral research at Oxford, followed by the chaplaincy of a large comprehensive school in the Shrewsbury Diocese. Then I had twelve years back at Oxford as a chaplain, where I also did some teaching as a member of the Theology Faculty. Once back in the Diocese, I became a school governor, and for five years was director of the Diocesan Religious Education Service before being posted to the Beda College in Rome as Rector, where I also taught various courses. And now I find myself at St Mary's University in Twickenham. There have been other commitments, but education has never been far away. In the large sense, it has had to be my line too. Many priests, not least through preaching and catechising, would be able to say the same.

Nevertheless, when people think about Newman and education, they are usually referring in particular to his book *The Idea of a University*, which has come to be regarded as a classic. One remarkable feature is the speed with which the nine lectures, which make up the essential core of the book, were written; so much else was happening to Newman at that time.

The background has become familiar. In April 1851, when Archbishop Cullen sent Newman a letter, asking for his advice about the proposed university in Ireland, he also suggested that, were Newman to visit, he might give some lectures. In the July he invited Newman to become the Rector and, between 10 May and 7 June the following year, Newman delivered the first five lectures. Two weeks later, from 21 to 24 June, the Achilli trial took place, in which he was found guilty, and three weeks after that, on 13 July, he preached to the newly restored hierarchy of Catholic Bishops of England and Wales one of his most famous sermons, 'The Second Spring' (*O.S.* pp. 163–82). Then, a mere three days later, on 16 July, his eldest sister Harriett died. They had been estranged for nine years because she believed, quite mistakenly, that he had been trying in 1843 to convert her husband to Roman Catholicism. Then, in the August, his aunt, Elizabeth, whom he loved dearly, also died.

In spite of everything, between the July and November of that year, 1852, he completed the text of four more lectures. Although they were never delivered, they were published. In the circumstances, the book is a *tour de force*, and the speed with which it was completed, in spite of the intense pressure involved, indicates Newman's mastery of his subject. But education has developed since then. How is Newman's *Idea* viewed today?

★

Those who have referred to *The Idea of a University* more recently have acknowledged its status as a classic, but they have also expressed their reservations. At Cambridge, for example, Professor Stefan Collini has warned people against deluding themselves that Newman's book 'describes an institution that at all closely resembles the universities we have today'. However, he adds that our twenty-first-century universities need a literary voice like Newman's, 'of comparable power to articulate in the idiom of our own time the ideal of the untrammelled quest for understanding'.[2]

Lord David Willetts, the former Minister for Universities and Science in the Coalition Government (2010–15), while criticising Newman for what he called the etymological mistake of arguing that universities should be devoted to the teaching of universal knowledge, has observed that 'perhaps that mistake contained a deeper truth and there is something universal about the university . . . We might hope that many graduates emerge able to fulfil Newman's ambition for them.'[3]

---

2 Stefan Collini, *What Are Universities for?* (London: Penguin, 2012), pp. 59–60.
3 David Willetts, *A University Education* (Oxford: Oxford University Press, 2017), pp. 14, 371–2.

NEWMAN: THE HEART OF HOLINESS

And back in 1990, the centenary year of Newman's death, the historian John Roberts, who had been Vice-Chancellor of Southampton University and then Warden of Merton College, Oxford, was invited to revisit and reassess Newman's *Idea*. While he too declared that the circumstances of universities today are 'utterly remote from the academic world taken for granted by Newman', he nevertheless described Newman's vision as one 'with which those of us who are concerned with education should from time to time try to refresh ourselves'. It is not a matter, Roberts noted, of forcing Newman's *Idea* to fit our needs, but of finding encouragement from him 'to defend values now under threat'.[4]

All these writers, of course, were emphasising principally the limitations, as they saw them, of Newman's *Idea* in today's circumstances. They were not praising Newman to the skies. Nevertheless, they were acknowledging that there is something in what he said that should be valued and protected.

★

At the very beginning of his lectures, Newman affirmed, 'The view taken of a University in these Discourses, is the following: – That it is a place of *teaching* universal *knowledge*' (*Idea*, p. ix [5]). Besides Lord Willetts' etymological concern, John Roberts took issue with this starting point. He found the claim that universities should teach all subjects implausible and impossible. He argued that it presupposed an unchanging culture that has become alien to our civilisation. How can a university seek to provide a comprehensive account of knowledge in a world like ours? 'For most students it is impossible fully to understand and make one subject their own,' he observed. 'To understand its interconnections with all others is

---

4 John M. Roberts, '*The Idea of a University* Revisited', in Ian Ker and Alan G. Hill (eds), *Newman after a Hundred Years*, pp. 220–1.

unimaginable.'[5] And in any case, he went on to argue, to possess truth at all it is not necessary to have the whole truth. Partial knowledge is often enough; it is not necessary to know everything in order to know something. It is not necessary to teach everything so that students can learn effectively. Must a university go on relentlessly adding subject after subject?

All this makes sense. Yet perhaps he was labouring the point. Was Newman necessarily saying anything more than that a university ought in principle to be open to teaching all subjects and by the same token in principle omitting none? While different disciplines are distinct and their distinctiveness must be respected, it can also be valuable to recognise what may connect them.

★

Roberts was writing in a collection of essays called *Newman after a Hundred Years* that came out in 1990, the centenary of Newman's death. However, that was not the only volume published in 1990 to commemorate that centenary. *Louvain Studies* also produced a special issue on Newman, which included a contribution by Nicholas Lash. He called his paper, '"A Seat of Wisdom, A Light of the World": Considering the University'.[6] Lash's key observations with regard to Newman's understanding of the university corresponded instructively with issues raised by Roberts, but he approached them from a different angle.

While Roberts, as we have noticed, drew attention to Newman's understanding of a university as a place where, in principle, all subjects would be taught, and believed that that was impossible and implausible, Lash laid emphasis instead on

5 Roberts, '*The Idea of a University* Revisited', p. 205.
6 Nicholas Lash, '"A Seat of Wisdom, A Light of the World": Considering the University', *Louvain Studies*, vol. 15, summer–autumn 1990, nn. 2–3, pp. 188–202.

the unity of truth and knowledge that those subjects unveil. He quoted Newman:

> All that exists, as contemplated by the human mind, forms one large system or complex fact, and this of course resolves itself into an indefinite number of particular facts, which, as being portions of a whole, have countless relations of every kind, one towards another. Knowledge is the apprehension of these facts, whether in themselves, or in their mutual positions and bearings.

Interconnectedness is crucial. The human mind struggles to take in such an array. Newman illustrated that struggle by producing one of those images that characterise his writing: 'Like a short-sighted reader, its eye [the eye of the human mind] pores closely, and travels slowly, over the awful volume which lies open for its inspection' (*Idea*, p. 45 [52, 53]).[7] Newman believed that there was a unity to the reality that sciences study, although they explore that reality 'under its various aspects' (*Idea*, p 47 [54]).

Lash then offered a swift sketch of the shift in intellectual focus over recent centuries, from the more objective approach during the seventeenth and eighteenth centuries to the more subjective in the nineteenth. Then, shortly afterwards, he observed, 'The twentieth century has seen, in several places, a further shift: towards the instrumentalism and pragmatism of "pure experience".'[8] This last comment in particular is borne out by an earlier remark of Roberts', with regard to Newman's reference to the 'bare idea' of a university, as 'almost the last thing British universities seek'. And he went on to explain why. Today's universities, he observed, are 'rooted in philo-sophical and intellectual incoherence. They are cluttered up with doctrinal and practical accretions, and are expected and

7 Lash, 'Considering the University', p. 191.
8 Lash, 'Considering the University', pp. 191, 193.

usually willing to do much more than provide intellectual training'. That they should be ready to offer more is admirable, but they are not looking for a single voice to speak for them. The system of which they are a part was, he wrote, 'pragmatically constructed' and 'historically conditioned'. Here is acknowledgment of the shift towards the pragmatism of 'pure experience', which met needs as they arose.[9]

There is, of course, much to be said for pragmatism. It can prevent us from becoming entangled in endless theorising. Nevertheless, when pragmatism dominates, it can lead to a fragmentation that undermines coherence, leading indeed, to repeat Roberts' phrase, to universities 'rooted in philosophical and intellectual incoherence'.

★

Pragmatism has become so important in universities today because students expect to be equipped for careers, supplied with the skills they need for success. They have come for a particular purpose and they want to get their money's worth. It is a viewpoint far removed from Newman's. When he was writing, a university was not preoccupied with utility, with what is useful, training people for employment. That preoccupation reduced a university, he believed, to 'a sort of bazaar, or pantechnicon, in which wares of all kinds are heaped together for sale in stalls independent of each other'. Instead, he praised knowledge as an end in itself and believed that 'a University is the home, it is the mansion-house, of the goodly family of the Sciences, sisters all, and sisterly in their mutual dispositions'.[10]

9 Roberts, 'The Idea of a University Revisited', pp. 196, 197; Idea, p. 125 [114].

10 Ker (ed.), The Idea of a University, p. 421. This passage occurs in the original fifth lecture that, for reasons that are still debated, Newman decided to omit from later editions. Ker included it in his critical edition as Appendix I.

So times have changed dramatically. The significance of a range of skills and training in education has come to be recognised and seen as valuable and well worthwhile. All the same, as Nicholas Lash has stressed, what unifies is also important. He wrote, echoing deliberately Newman's phrase:

> The university, 'taken in its bare idea', is not a collection of libraries and lecture-rooms, departments and faculties, seminars and field-trips, playing fields and late-night resolutions of the problems of mankind. The 'idea' of a university is that one unifying formal feature or aspect of those things which explains and justifies the university's existence and its purposes when considered precisely in abstraction from the myriad activities, institutions and enterprises which go (materially) to make it up.[11]

At the same time, there is no incompatibility between a unifying idea and more specialised teaching. Newman himself was delighted by his School of Medicine in Dublin: 'What indeed can it [a university] teach at all, if it does not teach something particular?' he exclaimed (*Idea*, p. 166 [145]). Nevertheless, as he had asserted earlier, a university essentially 'educates the intellect to reason well in all matters, to reach towards truth, and to grasp it'. And here he added, 'a cultivated intellect, because it is a good in itself, brings with it a power and a grace to every work and occupation which it undertakes, and enables us to be more useful, and to a greater number' (*Idea*, pp. 126 [114], 167 [146]).

And yet it is necessary to probe more deeply. Where is the unifying factor to be located? Wherever it may be, in Roberts' view it will not be in religion. Yet Nicholas Lash drew attention to an article Newman wrote for the Dublin *Catholic University Gazette* in 1854, as the university was opening

11 Lash, 'Considering the University', p. 196.

formally. He called it, 'What is a University?' There Newman made use of the close analogy between the idea of a university and the idea of the Church. He declared, 'In the nature of things, greatness and unity go together; excellence implies a centre.' And Lash supported Ian Ker's observation that Newman likened Church and university 'to political organisms, where the many individuals are brought into unity not uniformity, and where the conflict of the various parts ensures and enhances their own vitality'.[12] Furthermore, Lash commented that both Church and university, 'in distinct ways, minister to that saving wisdom, that healing of humankind in truth, which is (according to the Fourth Gospel) the true enlightenment of a darkened world'.[13] Indeed, Newman's words at this juncture supply Lash with the title for his article: Newman described a university as 'a seat of wisdom, a light of the world, a minister of the faith, an Alma Mater of the rising generation' (H.S. iii. p. 16).

What is needed, Lash went on to argue, is a way to recapture a 'sense of the *interdependence* of all the elements of that "one large and complex fact" which all things constitute'. A recognition of that interdependence is vital. And a real, rather than a notional, apprehension of the interrelatedness of things, he continued, 'calls for something other than mere erudition or intelligence or particular skill: it calls for a "philosophical habit," for something more like wisdom'. And while philosophy rather than wisdom was the expression favoured by Newman, Lash preferred wisdom, because, as he explained persuasively, philosophy today 'too readily suggests a particular discipline or subject, something in which students may be set examinations by persons acknowledged to be expert in the field. And this was not at all what Newman had in mind.'[14]

12 Ker (ed.), *Idea*, p. lxxv.
13 Lash, 'Considering the University', p. 198.
14 Lash, 'Considering the University', pp. 199–200, 201.

So what did Newman have in mind? Perhaps it can be found in one of the sermons he preached as Rector in Dublin. He delivered a series in 1856 and 1857, the first of which was called 'Intellect, the Instrument of Religious Training' (O.S. pp. 1–14). Although he had made it clear in *The Idea of a University* that what he had been attempting in those lectures was 'not contemplating . . . the characteristics of a University which is Catholic, but inquiring what a University is, what is its aim, what its nature, what its bearings' (*Idea*, p. 214 [183]), here, towards the end of the sermon, he spoke of the Catholic Church's objective when setting up universities, like the one in Dublin. It is seeking, he said, 'to reunite things which were in the beginning joined together by God, and have been put asunder by man'.

So interconnectedness was essential. That may sound today like interference or even censorship. But he continued immediately, 'Some people will say I am thinking of confining, distorting, and stunting the growth of the intellect by ecclesiastical supervision. I have no such thought.' Nor was he advocating some kind of compromise: 'Nor have I any thought of a compromise, as if religion must give up something, and science something.' Having cleared the ground, he set out his stall in style:

I wish the intellect to range with the utmost freedom, and religion to enjoy an equal freedom; but what I am stipulating for is, that they should be found in one and the same place, and exemplified in the same persons. I want to destroy that diversity of centres, which puts everything into confusion by creating a contrariety of influences. I wish the same spots and the same individuals to be at once oracles of philosophy and shrines of devotion. It will not satisfy me, what satisfies so many, to have two independent systems, intellectual and religious, going at once side by side, by a sort of division of labour, and only accidentally brought together. It will not satisfy me, if religion is here, and science there, and young men converse with

124

science all day, and lodge with religion in the evening. It is not touching the evil, to which these remarks have been directed, if young men eat and drink and sleep in one place, and think in another: I want the same roof to contain both the intellectual and moral discipline.

He was affirming the integrity of both disciplines, intellectual and moral, and he concluded famously:

Devotion is not a sort of finish given to the sciences; nor is science a sort of feather in the cap, if I may so express myself, an ornament and set-off to devotion. I want the intellectual layman to be religious, and the devout ecclesiastic to be intellectual (*O.S.* pp. 12–13).

Here, again, his incarnational vision was evident, the intellectual and the moral, the secular and the sacred, the seen and the unseen, united to the benefit of them both.

Furthermore, Newman did not wish people simply to be well read. A great memory, he noted in his lectures, 'does not make a philosopher, any more than a dictionary can be called a grammar. There are men who embrace in their minds a vast multitude of ideas, but with little sensibility about their real relations towards each other'. Yet:

the intellect which has been disciplined to the perfection of its powers, which knows, and thinks while it knows, which has learned to leaven the dense mass of facts and events with the elastic force of reason, such an intellect cannot be partial, cannot be exclusive, cannot be impetuous, cannot be at a loss, cannot but be patient, collected, and majestically calm, because it discerns the end in every beginning, the origin in every end, the law in every interruption, the limit in each delay; because it ever knows where it stands, and how its path lies from one point to another (*Idea*, pp. 135 [121], 138 [123–4]).

Those who are wise have done more than accumulate large quantities of information. They recognise the links and connections between what they know. Newman was explicit that he was not referring to genius, but to what he described as that 'perfection of the Intellect, which is the result of education . . . the clear, calm, accurate vision and comprehension of all things, as far as the finite mind can embrace them, each in its own place, and with its own characteristics upon it' (*Idea*, pp. 138–9 [124]).

★

Education is always controversial. Ways of understanding how people are to be educated evolve continually. Newman's commitment to education and his talent for educating were wide ranging. He saw educating as fundamental to his ministry and his way of life. It was, in the large sense, his line. But tertiary education today is far removed from what it was in Newman's time. In noticing here, however, some of the more recent criticism to which his ideas about the university have been subjected, certain strands of his thought may still be acknowledged as valuable, not least in the light of dissatisfaction with the fragmented narrative which is the consequence of more intense specialisation. And two features of Newman's approach remain particularly significant: first, that there is a unity that binds all knowledge together; and second, that that unity involves a unifying thread, relationships, an interconnectedness which may indeed be called wisdom.

The outline of intellectual history, sketched acutely by Nicholas Lash, has alerted us to a movement from the objective to the subjective and then on to the pragmatic, a shift that is acknowledged in John Roberts' reflections. That is where we have come to. But is it actually where we wish to be?

David Willetts, too, in summing up his study on university education, referred to the bleak analyses that are on display: 'It is not just worries about funding or intrusive university admin-istration,' he remarked. 'It is a deeper anxiety that the univer-sity is "in ruins" because there is no longer any coherent account of it in our post-modern world.'[15] Incoherence domi-nates. Willetts says he does not share this gloomy view, but he recognises that it is current. It has become the fashion. However, we need to recognise that there is a unity to knowl-edge and to recognise what we have in common, what unites us, what bonds bind us together, where there is connection and relationship.

John Roberts, as we have seen, was rather sceptical about enlarging the range of studies a university might offer, but Newman was enthusiastic. He was not being naïve. He recog-nised that students could not pursue every subject, but he was convinced all the same that they would gain 'by living among those and under those who represent the whole circle'. And he declared:

> This I conceive to be the advantage of a seat of universal learn-ing, considered as a place of education. An assemblage of learned men, zealous for their own sciences, and rivals of each other, are brought, by familiar intercourse and for the sake of intellectual peace, to adjust together the claims and relations of their respective subjects of investigation. They learnt to respect, to consult, to aid each other. Thus is created a pure and clear atmosphere of thought, which the student also breathes, though in his own case he only pursues a few sciences out of the multitude (*Idea*, p. 101 [95]).

What Newman was describing may be dismissed as an ideal beyond us, living, as we do, in times that are governed by market forces, where students at universities want to be equipped for a career and so are keen to concentrate upon

15 Willetts, *A University Education*, p. 370.

specialising, acquiring expertise for future success. Yet excessive specialisation creates fragmentation. The interaction of disciplines, their interconnectedness, is precisely a key value that needs to be protected. It is in particular an essential aspect of Catholic education.

The matter was stated clearly some years ago by Father James Heft, Professor of Religion at the University of Southern California, when he affirmed that 'the Catholic intellectual tradition seeks to integrate knowledge'. He continued, 'There ought to be connections between all the subjects studied because everything that is studied has its source, ultimately, in God.' Non-believers will not agree, and Heft acknowledged that the task is daunting, given the expansion of knowledge in the past hundred years. All the same, he insisted that 'Catholic universities must resist the fragmentation of knowledge typical of secular universities. Scholars who rely exclusively on already established methodologies within their disciplines will prematurely dismiss important questions they don't yet know how to answer.'[16]

Let me offer a personal experience in a minor key. As Catholic chaplain at Oxford during the 1980s I was invited regularly to preach at evensong in different colleges. One day, one of the dons surprised me by remarking that he envied me my knowledge of the university. I was taken aback. But he then explained that, in the past, a new fellow or lecturer would be invited by colleagues in the same faculty to dine in their colleges; it was how they came to know one another and meet a range of people who were experts in different disciplines. Now, however, he lamented, with increased bureaucracy and more faculty meetings, they saw so much of each other in any case that those invitations had largely lapsed. He regretted the loss.

16 See James L. Heft, 'Distinctively Catholic: Keeping the Faith in Higher Education', *Commonweal*, 22 March 2010, pp. 10–11.

Newman's *Idea of a University* is not an immutable guide to university education. Times have changed. But Newman had a talent for educating, and that talent and the book he wrote can continue to challenge universities today. In particular, it can stir them to recognise the way different disciplines may, after all, be related. In other words, they may rediscover coherence. And by that rediscovery they may be able to resist fragmentation more effectively and so defend those values that at present are under threat. His legacy may still be greater than we realise.

10

An apologia for our times

We are drawing to a close. Recognising from the start Newman's sense of the link between what is seen and what is unseen, his awareness of the relationship between the visible and the invisible, we have been trying gradually to peel back the layers to uncover his spiritual life and vision. What model of holiness does he offer us? What path was he following? As he believed that the very definition of a Christian is someone who looks for Christ, we have considered the way he sought to be alert to Christ's presence, and then we have explored his understanding of the Christ as one, as divine, and as human, an understanding that he approached in a way that was keenly sensitive to the mystery he was contemplating.

This wonder before the mystery led him to rejoice in the gift of the Eucharist and inspired him as he prayed. But it did not shield him from darkness, or dreariness, as he called it, or his sense at times of personal failure. All this relates to the inner man. But, at the same time, he was never a recluse: from his election as a fellow of Oriel and his leadership of the Oxford Movement to the projects he undertook as a Catholic and his declining years as a cardinal, we have found that pastoral ministry remained integral to everything he did, exercised most notably, of course, through his talent for educating. That was his path. And so, we may now ask, where has it left us? What is Newman's legacy? Perhaps we may see it as an apologia for our times.

An apologia, we must remember, is not an apology. It is rather an explanation, and a particular kind of explanation, not one that claims brashly to be right and dismisses all others as wrong. Instead it commends its viewpoint as an alternative, offering it in this instance as a wiser and richer vision for human society and its future than the version inspired by alternatives, and so, today in particular, the contemporary sway of the secular.

Why do we need such an apologia? Besides the polemics of the self-proclaimed atheists like Richard Dawkins and Christopher Hitchens with their relentless, ultimately unpersuasive negativity because they seem to be blind to anything good in Christianity, there is a far more significant issue. It is that view of the world, prevalent today, to use Newman's phrase, as 'a world simply irreligious'. He used the expression in a sermon he preached in 1873, called 'The Infidelity of the Future'. He envisaged a time when the Church would be facing what he called 'a darkness different in kind from any that has been seen before it', a time when, for example, as its influence increases, the Church will be handicapped by 'scandals from the misconduct of its members'. And, he added, 'we are at the mercy of even one unworthy member'.[1] There will always be such people in a large body.

If that time had not already come during Newman's lifetime, we know well that it has come now, at least in much of western society, with the Church mired in scandal and its credibility shot to pieces, not by one unworthy member, but by so many. In these circumstances, what response can be made? How might Newman be of help? What might we learn from him? What alternative does he suggest? We have to revisit the path he took.

★

That path began with his awareness of the intimate link between what is seen and what is unseen as being revealed

---

1 *Catholic Sermons of Cardinal Newman*, pp. 123, 121, 128–9.

supremely in Jesus of Nazareth, who is the Christ. This conviction was not naïve piety. In those sermons in 1836, both the
unpublished and published, we found that he offered an understanding of the Christ as the person in whom the human and
the divine were fully present and perfectly united. For example, he spoke of Christ being 'as entirely man as if he had
ceased to be God, as fully God as if he had never become man,
as fully both at once as He was in being at all' (*P.S.* vi, p. 66).
This understanding related not only to the Christ, but became
moreover the basis for his vision of human holiness.

In one of the Dublin sermons that he preached in 1857,
while he was Rector of the university, he reflected on what he
referred to as 'St Paul's Characteristic Gift'. He began by distin-
guishing two kinds of holiness. There are some indeed, he
suggested, who are 'so absorbed in the divine life, that they
seem, even while they are in the flesh, to have no part in earth
or in human nature' (*O.S.* pp. 91–2). He mentioned, for example, mystics and the Desert Fathers. But then, he went on,
there are others:

> in whom the supernatural combines with nature, instead of
> superseding it, – invigorating it, elevating it, ennobling it; . . .
> who are not less men, because they are saints. They do not put
> away their natural endowments, but use them to the glory of
> the Giver; they do not act beside them, but through them; they
> do not eclipse them by the brightness of divine grace, but only
> transfigure them. They are versed in human society; they
> understand the human heart; they can throw themselves into
> the minds of other men; and all this in consequence of natural
> gifts and secular education . . . The world is to them a book, to
> which they are drawn for its own sake, which they read fluently,
> which interests them naturally . . . Thus they have the thoughts,
> feelings, frames of mind, attractions, sympathies, antipathies of
> other men, so far as these are not sinful, only they have these
> properties of human nature purified, sanctified, and exalted;

and they are only made more eloquent, more poetical, more profound, more intellectual, by reason of their being more holy (O.S. pp. 92–3).

The most illuminating sentence for me declares, 'The world is to them a book, to which they are drawn for its own sake, which they read fluently, which interests them naturally.' It captures so precisely the integrity of the secular and the sacred and their union. And among those he mentions drawn to this book which they read fluently and naturally, we find his great hero, Athanasius, and, of course, the apostle Paul. It is his characteristic gift.

What Newman was proposing is a profoundly incarnational vision of holiness in which the two partners, what is of grace and what is human, are distinct from, but perfectly in tune with, each other. And this incarnational vision is not confined to some kind of private, interior spiritual life. The pattern can be found reflected as well in his understanding of education, influencing his talent for educating. In an earlier sermon in the same series that we have already noticed, he declared:

> it will not satisfy me, what satisfies so many, to have two independent systems, intellectual and religious, going at once side by side, by a sort of division of labour, and only accidentally brought together . . . I want the same roof to contain both the intellectual and moral discipline.

And then came the famous conclusion about wanting the intellectual layman to be religious and the devout ecclesiastic to be intellectual (see O.S. pp. 12–13). Their unity is integral to their being authentic. So it is of the essence of this alliance between the human and the divine, the secular and the sacred, each distinct, yet in union, that neither threatens the other, but each is enhanced by their being united. Secularists should not be dismayed by this vision. They may not be able to accept it, but they should not dismiss it out of hand. John Harriott, the gifted writer and broadcaster, challenged those who do shortly before he died in 1990: 'Argue by all means that the believer's universe is a delusion,' he wrote, 'but not that a vision of human life stretching beyond time and space is smaller than one that sees it ending in a handful of dust.'[2] He was in effect echoing Newman's vision.

★

To share this conviction of Newman's, however, and to reach beyond the secular to embrace the sacred is not to discover a panacea that offers protection from all trouble, distress and disaster. Newman's own experience makes that plain.

As we have seen, he was highly regarded. He was a priest of the established Church, the Church of England, and a fellow of Oriel College, at a time when that college was famous among Oxford colleges for its academic excellence. He was the vicar of the university church, a renowned preacher and, with Edward Pusey and John Keble, the influential leader within the Anglican Church of the Tractarian Movement, which was accomplishing more than they had initially dared to imagine.

All had seemed set fair for success, but then, as we know, he was led by events and his own arguments to doubt the position in which he had felt so secure. His world collapsed around him. After careful study, in obedience to conscience, he left the Church of England to become a Catholic. It is difficult to grasp now the magnitude of that decision in the eyes of his contemporaries. He had abandoned a position of honour and prestige to join a small, despised minority.

Many people regarded him with contempt. Was he a traitor or a fool? While some friendships endured, many others did not. Pusey kept in touch, but even as dear and saintly a friend

2 Quoted by Hugo Young, *The Tablet*, 5 January 1991.

as John Keble made no contact with him for seventeen years. When he finally wrote to ask Newman's pardon, his letter was moving, and Newman replied, 'Never have I doubted for one moment your affection for me – never have I been hurt at your silence' (*L.D.* xx, pp. 501–3 [355]). Their friendship was resumed. But there had been many an anguished parting of ways.

And did the Catholic community that he had joined make up for what he had lost? We know it did not. Catholics in many ways were bewildered to have so distinguished a man in their midst. Some were suspicious, and those in authority were unsure how to make best use of him. We recall again that succession of projects he was invited to undertake, but in which each time he was thwarted by a lack of support, and sometimes by direct personal hostility. It seemed as though everything he turned his hand to ended in disaster.

That long, dark journal entry in January 1863, to which we have often referred, makes sombre reading. 'O how forlorn & dreary has been my course since I have been a Catholic!' he wrote. He was aware that he had come to look stern:

how am I changed even in look! till the affair of No 90 and my going to Littlemore, I had my mouth half open, and commonly a smile on my face – and from that time onwards my mouth has been closed and contracted, and the muscles are so set now, that I cannot but look grave and forbidding.

Then, with probably unintended humour, he related an incident in Rome with his companion, Bernard Dalgairns:

Even as early as 1847, when I was going through the Vatican with Dalgairns, stopping before a statue of Fate, which was very striking and stern and melancholy, he said, 'Who *can* it be like? I know the face so well' – presently he added, 'Why, it is you.'

Newman continued:

> It began when I set my face towards Rome; and, since I made the great sacrifice, to which God called me, He has rewarded me in ten thousand ways, O how many! but he has marked my course with almost unintermittent mortification.

The depressive tone gathers:

> Few indeed successes has it been His blessed will to give me through life. I doubt whether I can point to any joyful event of this world besides my scholarship at Trinity & my fellowship at Oriel.

And it was here that he concluded, 'since I have been a Catholic, I seem to myself to have had nothing but failure, personally' (*A.W.* pp. 254–5).

A year later, of course, came Kingsley's aside that led to Newman writing his *Apologia pro Vita Sua*, which helped change many people's perception of him. But his troubles were not over. There were further trials to come, such as the dispute with regard to the Oxford Oratory and the anxiety and controversy surrounding the definition of papal infallibility. But then, in 1879, to Newman's astonishment, Pope Leo XIII decided to make him a cardinal.

The Pope's action in its way changed everything. It lifted the cloud that had hung over him, the suspicion that he was an unreliable Catholic. As he told his friend, Mother Mary Imelda Poole, 'It is a wonderful Providence, that even before my death that acquittal of me comes, which I knew would come some day or other, though not in my life time' (*L.D.* xxix, p. 63). The final years then became more tranquil.

Newman's life was beset with trials and sufferings. They may not have been as obviously dramatic or spectacular as those of famous martyrs, but they were often severe, and they wounded him deeply. He knew well the experience of desolation that is an inescapable part of human living. Indeed, in 1837, at the height of his fame in Oxford, he preached a sermon that contained a sentence which seems, quite remarkably, to predict what his life was to become. He declared, 'The planting of Christ's Cross in the heart is sharp and trying; but the stately tree rears itself aloft, and has fair branches and rich fruit, and is good to look upon' (*P.S.* iv, p. 262).

No one lives a life entirely untouched by trials and challenges. Some people suffer physically, perhaps because of a disability that handicaps them, or on account of an accident that has occurred, or because they are caught up in some disaster, whether natural, like flood or famine, or man-made, when they are victims of crime or are refugees caught up in a war zone. Then there are others for whom life has been a disappointment: their career has failed, or they have been misjudged. There are those who have been wounded by broken friendships and failed relationships. And which of us has not been bereaved? The list could go on and on.

Some people become obsessed with these experiences, clinging to them, refusing to let them go. Their plight is tragic, because they let their sorrow smother them. An apologia for our times needs to offer a response to those trials. It calls for more than stubborn endurance. It must rather encourage a readiness to plant generously the tree of the cross in our own hearts so as to let it put down deep roots. Then, when we have done so, we will realise how that stately tree grows tall, bears fruit and catches the eye. Fidelity is the key. By embracing hardship generously and remaining faithful, as Newman did, we may discover and bear witness to the way disaster may be turned into triumph. What had seemed like dying is transformed into new life.

★

If a recognition of the relationship between the sacred and the secular is one feature of Newman's legacy, as we seek to fashion an apologia for our times, an alternative to the viewpoint championed by secularism alone, and if to remain steadfast in the face of trials so as to find new life is another, there is also a third feature in Newman's thinking that can be of help.

Wilfrid Ward, who wrote that first major biography of Newman, included a sentence from a letter that Newman had written to him late in life: 'The religious mind sees much which is invisible to the irreligious mind. They have not the same evidence before them.'[3] Ward was probably paraphrasing Newman's letter to him of 20 December 1884, in which he observed that 'a religious mind must always master much which is unsure to the irreligious; . . . I can't allow that a religious man has no more evidence *necessarily*, than a non-religious' (*L.D.* xxx, p. 446). What, then, is extra for the religious mind? Was the old man just engaging in special pleading? Yet these words of his seem to dovetail with something St Paul once wrote.

In his First Letter to the Corinthians Paul told them:

Now we have received not the spirit of the world, but the Spirit that is from God, so that we may understand the gifts bestowed on us by God. And we speak of these things in words not taught by human wisdom but taught by the Spirit, interpreting spiritual things to those who are spiritual (1 Corinthians 2:12–13).

In other words, he was saying, we have received not the spirit of the world, but the Spirit that is from God, and we have received that Spirit for a purpose: *so that* we may understand the gifts God has bestowed on us. And then, when we speak about them, we do so, he was telling us, not just in ordinary words, but in words taught by the Spirit: we teach spiritual things to those who are in tune with the Spirit. Paul, we might

3 Ward, *The Life of John Henry Cardinal Newman*, ii, p. 247.

say, was sketching a whole psychological dynamic of faith: the presence of the Spirit enables those who have received the Spirit to understand the gifts of the Spirit and to explain and interpret those gifts to those who are attuned to receive them.

If that all seems rather complex, let me offer an analogy. Many years ago there was a television programme called *Badger Watch*. Shy creatures, badgers usually come out only under cover of darkness, when they cannot be seen. The darkness hides them. They might not be there at all. The programme was made possible, of course, because, although these creatures were invisible to the naked human eye, with the aid of the appropriate light – an infra-red light – the camera's eye was able to see them. When I saw this programme, it occurred to me how this filming offered a kind of analogy for what Paul and Newman were describing. To the unaided human mind in search of spiritual truth, like the naked human eye looking for badgers, there is nothing there. All is darkness. But as the infra-red light assists the camera's eye, so the light of the Spirit brings light to the unaided mind and enables the eye of faith to detect and see what otherwise would be hidden, but which indeed is there.

There is no special pleading here. It is a matter of recognising that there is a perceptiveness appropriate to believing, as there is an ear appropriate for appreciating music and an eye for appreciating art. Years ago I knew a kind woman of very definite opinions (she has since died) who once declared authoritatively and dismissively, 'I've no time for music.' Then, after a brief pause, she admitted sweetly, 'Of course, I've no ear for it.' The religious mind sees much that is invisible to the irreligious mind.

We need to cultivate the perceptiveness appropriate to faith, if we are to offer an alternative viewpoint, an apologia for our time. Faith, as Newman once observed, is not the reasoning of a weak mind, but 'the reasoning of a divinely enlightened one' (*U.S.* p. 208 [147]). How we achieve that enlightenment, how we live and how we pray, will vary from person to person. As St John of the Cross once explained, 'God carries each person along a different road, so that you will scarcely find two people following the same route in even half of their journey to God.'[4] Some will be more active, some will sing psalms, some will read reflectively, others will lapse into silence, and Newman, as we have learnt, prayed best with a pen in his hand.

★

We have covered a lot of ground, yet it may seem that we have scarcely begun. What in the first place we have learnt from Newman about the relationship between the secular and the sacred, and then about the movement from darkness to light, from desolation to peace, from death to new life, is not offered as a simplistic recipe. There is much more that needs to be considered. Nevertheless, in the face of relentless secularism, to embrace the sacred with the secular and to move with generous hearts from darkness into the light creates an apologia that offers hope.

When I reflect on these matters, particularly in the context of Newman as a saint, it occurs to me that the relationship between the sacred and the secular is what is celebrated at Christmas, the Word becoming flesh and dwelling among us; and that the movement from darkness to light, from death to new life, is what we commemorate during Lent and Eastertide – the passion, death, and resurrection of Jesus. This apologia, the alternative to which Newman points, is not, of course, achieved without effort, but I am encouraged to find that it corresponds to these major feasts. Moreover, if we are wise and remain open to the possibility that the religious mind, as Newman told Wilfrid Ward, does indeed see much that is

4 John of the Cross, *Living Flame of Love*, stanza 3. 59; quoted in Iain Matthew, *The Impact of God* (London: Hodder & Stoughton, Ltd., 1995), p. 15.

invisible to the irreligious, then we are being alert to the Spirit whose presence we celebrate at the third great feast, that of Pentecost.

Such openness, lived faithfully, may then help to reveal and restore trust in the gospel's vision. As it was for Newman, education in the large sense is the line to be taken. And yet at the same time, crafting this apologia, it is vital never to forget the words of Pope St Paul VI that, 'Modern man listens more willingly to witnesses than to teachers, and if he does listen to teachers, it is because they are witnesses.'[5] Those who want to promote this viewpoint are called to be witnesses of gospel truth and love; they are being invited to move out of the shadows into the truth, *ex umbris et imaginibus in veritatem*.

So we will let Newman have the final word. He was speaking of the great Athanasius – although we may apply the same words to him – and we can hope as well that little by little they may be applied also to us: 'after all, say they are few, such high Christians; and what follows? They are enough to carry on God's noiseless work' (*U.S.* p. 96 [75]).

5 Pope Paul VI, *Evangelii Nuntiandi*, n. 41.

Index

Ward, W. G. xviii–xix, 3, 11, 12

'Watching' (Newman) 33–4
Whately, Richard 72
Wilberforce, Henry 59–60
Wilberforce, Samuel 72, 104
Wilfridians 106

Willetts, Lord David 117, 126–7
Williams, Lord Rowan 46
Wiseman, Cardinal Nicholas 4,
   7, 86–9, 96
Wootten, Frances 110
Wordsworth, William 66–7